Endpapers, Large Munsterlanders; page 1,
Norfolk Terrier; 2–3, Rhodesian
Ridgebacks; 4–5, Beagle.

Dogs

Dogs

Wendy Boorer

Royce
PUBLICATIONS

Contents

First published in Great Britain by Sundial Books Ltd
and distributed by Marks & Spencer Ltd

This edition published by Treasure Press
59 Grosvenor Street
London W1

© 1979 Hennerwood Publications Ltd

ISBN 0 907812 11 2

Printed in Hong Kong

Dogs of the past

The dog is believed to have been man's first success in domesticating a wild animal, although we cannot state with certainty where and when this association began. It probably started in the stage of man's history when he was still a nomadic tribal hunter and packs of scavenging wild dogs followed the wandering tribes to pick over the remains after a kill. These dogs would have provided an early warning system of the presence of large predators feared by man and dogs alike, and would also have been useful for scenting game before man would be aware of its existence. The first step towards domesticating was taken when man actively used dogs to help him hunt.

Once he was convinced that dogs

Left: *The Spitz breeds are found all over the world and are among the oldest types of dog.*

Below: *All modern dog breeds are believed to have descended from ancestors that looked like this Asian wild dog.*

had a use, man might very well have abducted puppies to rear himself, since semi-tame animals would be of greater assistance than their wilder relatives. Such dogs could be encouraged to find wounded animals and then hold them at bay, and eventually to precede the hunters in tracking game. Undoubtedly these early dogs were killed and eaten when game was scarce and also acted as a source of warmth to their owners. Today's pet, sleeping on the foot of the bed, has a long tradition behind it.

When man began to keep flocks and herds of grazing animals, the dog became a necessary and effective guard against wild predators. By harnessing and adapting the instincts of a hunting dog, man turned it into a herding animal too. Today, nearly all the movements of a sheepdog working sheep are those of a predator stalking prey; it is only the final dash and kill that is absent.

It is not known for certain what these early hunting dogs looked like,

The New Anubis

All along the moorland road a caravan there comes
Where the piping curlew whistles and the brown snipe drums;
And a long lean dog
At a sling jig-jog,
A poacher to his eyelids, as all the lurcher clan,
Follows silent as a shadow, and clever as a man.

His master on the splash-board, oh, of ancient race he is;
He came down out of Egypt, as did all the Romanys;
With a hard hawk face
Of an old king race,
His hair is black and snaky, and his cheek is brown as tea,
And pyramids and poacher-dogs are made by such as he.

Now the dog he looks as solemn as the beak upon the bench,
But he'll pounce and pick a hare up, and he'll kill it with a
    wrench,
Or he'll sneak around a rick
And bring back a turkey chick;
And you'll wonder how they got all his cock-a-leerie fakes.
Well, his master comes of people who turn walking sticks
    to snakes!

There was once a god in Egypt, when the gods they first began,
With the muzzle of a lurcher on the body of a man;
But the Pharaoh of to-day
He has changed the ancient way,
And has found him a familiar by his caravan to jog
With the head piece of a Solomon, the body of a dog!

Patrick C Chalmers

but it is probable that they were of a Spitz type, with a wedge-shaped head, pricked ears and a bushy tail, similar to their wild relatives. Dogs of this type appear to have long had a world-wide distribution.

The civilizations of the Middle East bred dogs with some care and selectivity, when the more primitive peoples of the north were still at a much earlier stage of development. Egyptian murals, from 4000 B.C. onwards, show domestication of several different types of greyhounds. One has a big upright bat ear like the modern Ibizan hound, while another has the small drop ear and the feathering of the modern Saluki. It is possible that a greyhound of some type, such as the Afghan, reached Afghanistan along the trade routes of the ancient world between the Middle

Above left: This picture from the Middle Ages shows the type of spaniel used to find game for hawks. Falconry was a fashionable pursuit for both sexes.

Left: The Welsh Springer Spaniel is a good working gundog on both land and water and is active and energetic.

East and China. It was discovered there by British Army Officers in the late nineteenth century, thereafter to be introduced to the western world.

The greyhound family were at their most successful in desert countries, where the hot, still air makes for bad scenting conditions, but excellent visibility. This suits all types of greyhounds, since they hunt by sight rather than scent and use speed to overtake their prey. For this reason, they are also known as gazehounds.

Early Assyrian wall paintings also portray a much larger, heavier dog with a blunt muzzle, reminiscent of a Mastiff. These were apparently used for hunting lions and were also taken into battle by their Assyrian masters. Dogs of this type may have reached Britain with the Phoenician traders who came for Cornish tin, bringing greyhounds and mastiffs with them. The Romans discovered the British Mastiff when they invaded this island and were so impressed by its size and ferocity that they sent several back to Rome to take part in the colourful gladiatorial displays.

The Middle Eastern peoples never

seem to have bred the hounds that hunt by scent, and indeed they would have no need for such animals. The scent hound evolved in cooler, milder climates, where the thickness of the vegetation would prevent a gazehound from seeing the game. The humidity of the countries further north provided good scenting conditions for dogs bred to follow a trail with the tenacity of purpose that would enable them to wear down their quarry. From the time of the peak of Greek civilization through to the European Middle Ages, hunting with packs of scent hounds was a passion with the nobility and its importance is reflected in the complicated and punitive game laws of this period.

Spaniel-type dogs are shown in use in mediaeval times finding and putting up birds for the sport of hawking and falconry, or pointing and flushing game into nets. From these animals, many of today's well-known gundog breeds are descended.

Not all dogs were valued solely for their usefulness, however. Toy dogs have always appealed to man and the mummified remains of very small dogs

9

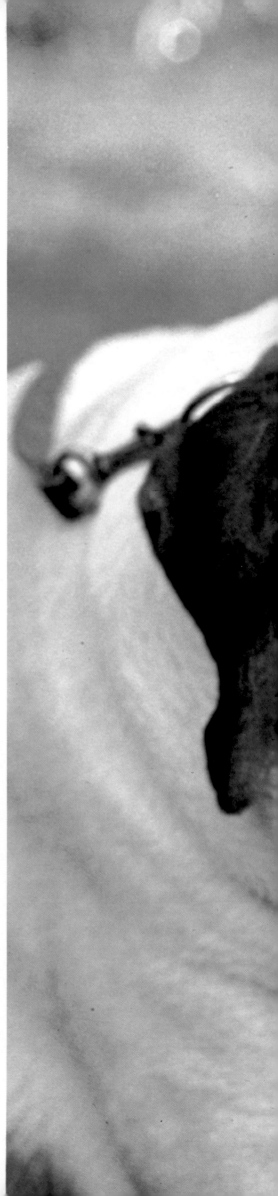

have been found in Egyptian tombs. The Chinese also bred small, flat-faced dogs from early times. The first of these to reach Europe was the Pug, brought by the Dutch and Portuguese who traded with Canton in the sixteenth century and considered the small dogs valuable curiosities. The breed reached Britain from Holland with the court of William of Orange and became a fashionable lady's dog.

Many of the working breeds of the past, as opposed to the hunting dogs, have an undocumented history, for they did not attract the attention of artists or writers. We know that the vermin-hunting terriers, the cattle-droving dogs and the sheepdogs have been in existence for centuries, but we know little about their appearance before the nineteenth century. Life would not have been possible in the Arctic until very recently without the use of the dog as a haulage animal. Draught dogs were also used in many other parts of the world and we know very little about these, too.

Although some dogs have been bred with care for specific purposes over many centuries, it was not until the advent of dog shows and the formation of the Kennel Club that pedigrees as records of ancestry became the universal general practice. The only dogs whose named ancestors are known before this are some packs of Foxhounds whose stud books go back to the eighteenth century. The first organized dog show in the world was held in Britain in 1858. Its success and popularity led to the formation of the Kennel Club in 1873. The Club's first positive action was to organize a stud book and only dogs registered in this were allowed to enter the shows which it then proceeded to organize. The purpose of this was to eliminate some of the unscrupulous malpractices and anarchy that reigned at the early shows. Nowadays, the Club exists mainly for the purpose of promoting dog shows, field trials, working trials, obedience tests and the overall improvement of dogs.

The transition of the role of the dog from a work animal to a pet is largely an event of the twentieth century. Before then, really the only dogs kept as pets were the various toy breeds, which have always been bred mainly as companions. Just why the dog became accepted into society primarily as a pet is hard to say; it may have been that as families became smaller, there became a greater need to keep animals as companions to counteract the loneliness induced by smaller family units.

Below: *Toy dogs have always had an appeal for man. Pugs are sturdy little dogs, originating from the Far East where the Chinese specialized in producing small dogs with flattened muzzles to be constant companions.*

Right: *The Old English Mastiff has a long and rather bloodthirsty history. The modern breed is a giant heavyweight with a dignified character.*

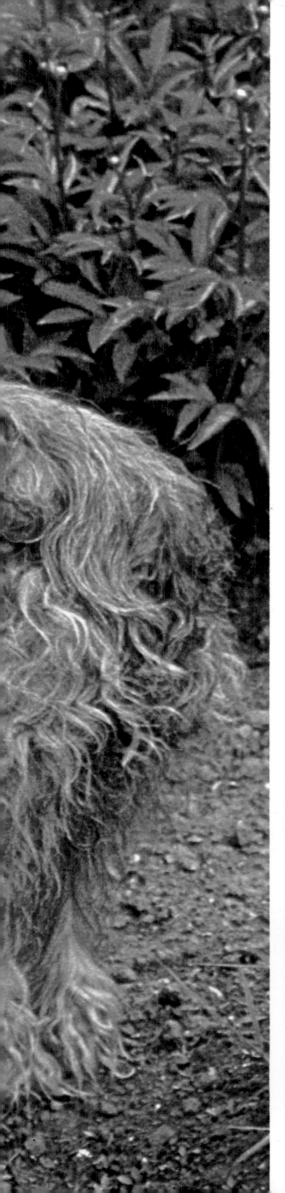

Town dog or country dog

Town dog or country dog, or any dog at all? A dog can be a comfort for the lonely, a guard for the home, an incentive to take the daily exercise necessary for health, a playmate for the young in heart and an outlet for the human need to love and care for some creature that will return affection with uncritical enthusiasm. These pleasures and benefits are generally taken for granted by dog lovers, but they entail a number of responsibilities which require objective consideration.

Bringing a dog into the household virtually amounts to adding another member to the family for the next ten years or so; a companion who lives for the moment and for whose behaviour you are responsible throughout every day. No dog should ever roam unsupervised, for one can never be completely sure that even the most

Left: *Despite their cumbersome appearance Old English Sheepdogs are active, energetic dogs.*

Below: *The English Pointer was bred to find game for the sportsman and to indicate the position of a bird.*

well-behaved pet is not fouling a pavement, causing a traffic accident, or joining some canine acquaintance to chivy and mutilate someone else's livestock. If your dog is not to be another person's nuisance then you must have time both to give the animal adequate exercise and some training in socially acceptable behaviour.

The dog's needs are fairly simple, but high on the list is companionship. Unlike cats, a dog is not a solitary animal by nature, so if it is to be left on its own all day or you live a highly social life and like the freedom of a weekend away at a moment's notice, choose a more accommodating pet. The happiest dogs are those who spend most of their waking life with their owners, especially if they are also called upon in some way to participate in their activities.

Dogs are an expense. They add to the household's food bill, they need veterinary attention at intervals and they need boarding accommodation during holidays. Furthermore, no household with a dog, just as no household with children, ever maintains that pristine, immaculate

The wonder ratter

TINY, the Wonder, weighing only 5½ lbs. Pedigree by Old Dick out of Old Nell. The property of James Shaw, Blue Anchor, Bonhill Row, St Luke's.

This extraordinary Black and Tan has won 50 interesting events, including the following matches: 2 matches of 6 rats when he weighed 4½ lbs; 20 matches of 12 rats at 5 lbs weight; 15 matches of 20 rats at 5 lbs weight; 1 match of 50 rats, 1 match of 100 rats in 34 minutes 40 seconds on Tuesday, March 30, 1847. Beat Summertown bitch 'Crack' of 8 lbs, 12 rats each, September 14. Beat the dog 'Twig' at 6½ lbs on November 7 and on Tuesday, March 28, 1848, he was matched to kill 300 rats in 3 hours; he accomplished the unprecedented test in 54 minutes 50 seconds, which took place in the presence of a crowded audience at the above house. May 2 – killed 20 rats in 8 minutes; May 23rd – won a match of 50 rats against Mr Batty's bitch 'Fun' 8 lbs; August 15 – won a match against 'Jim' 50 rats; September 5 won a match of 12 rats, 2 minutes 30 seconds; October 24 – won a match of 50 rats, time of killing 20 minutes 10 seconds; November 4 – won a match of 100 rats, 30 minutes 5 seconds; January 31, 1849 – won a match of 100 rats, 20 minutes 5 seconds; March 27 – killed 200 rats, 59 minutes 58 seconds. The above extraordinary feats were accomplished without either taking dogs or rats out of the pit.

Old handbill

state which some people consider necessary. An adequately fenced garden or somewhere for the dog to relieve itself without causing annoyance to others is essential, although it should be understood that leaving a dog out in the garden, where it will potter around on its own, is not a substitute for suitable exercise.

If after considering these points, you still want a dog, you must then decide what age, sex and breed or type of dog would best suit you. If buying a puppy, it is best to do so when it is about eight weeks old so that it can be integrated and gradually educated to be an acceptable member of its new family. Adult dogs sometimes need new homes through no fault of their own, but it is wise to check the dog's background and temperament in such cases. Taking on someone else's misfit can be a liability rather than an asset.

If you buy a pedigree puppy, you will know the size and appearance that it will have as an adult. To an extent, you will also know something about the temperament you can expect. With a mongrel puppy, however, all these things are a gamble. Even if you know its parents, it may very well turn out to be quite unlike either of them. The choice of a male or female animal is a matter of personal preference. The male dog is often bolder and more independent by nature, but can also be more aggressive and likely to want to roam. Bitches are generally more affectionate and home-loving but have the great disadvantage of coming into season about twice a year. Each time there is a three-week period during which they are 'on heat', which makes them very attractive to male dogs. Being on heat starts with a blood-stained discharge from the vagina which clears to a straw colour at about the tenth day. At this stage the bitch is not only ready to be mated but will actively seek a suitor. Her scent enables male dogs to track her to her door and they are persistent, cunning and often vocal admirers. It is possible to postpone or suppress a bitch's season with tablets from the veterinary surgeon, or alternatively you can have her spayed, an operation

Above left: *Blue Great Danes are a giant breed, requiring a lot of space and money for their upkeep.*

Right: *These Norwegian Buhund puppies belong to the Spitz group of breeds.*

which involves the removal of the ovaries and the uterus. This is major surgery and therefore costly. It should not be done until the bitch has had at least one season and is mature, otherwise she may experience adverse side effects, such as obesity. In addition, a bitch spayed too young, may also retain some puppy characteristics, which are generally not desirable in an adult dog.

Having considered the needs of a pet in relation to your own circumstances, try to decide what you want from a dog. Although generalizations about breed characteristics can be misleading when discussing individual animals, knowledge of the breed's original use is often some guide to the kind of temperament you can expect. By taking this into account, it may be possible to avoid such mistakes as buying a noisy extrovert when what you really want is a placid, comfort-loving, quiet companion.

Many people want to know if a dog will be good with children. Most dogs that grow up with a family are excellent with the younger generation, although it is important that the children are taught that an animal should never be teased or hurt. However, it is better to choose a placid breed than an excitable one that can get too carried away with rough and noisy games. To have a puppy when there is a toddler in the house is not really fair to either of them. The puppy's games will be too rough and the child will be too young to appreciate what will hurt or frighten a dog. Adult dogs that are unused to children often find them disturbing.

The following generalizations may be helpful in deciding what kind of dog is best for you. The gazehounds, or greyhound family, are built on galloping lines. They make dignified and gentle house dogs but the instinct to chase and kill can be triggered off by the sight of a small, moving object in the distance and in pursuit of anything they are virtually unstoppable. The scent hounds, originally bred to live and work in packs, are surprisingly sociable, friendly and non-aggressive types. However, they can be obstinate and conveniently deaf when following their own interests. All hounds can take practically unlimited exercise.

The giant breeds need a lot of money and space for their upkeep. Usually they do not need as much exercise as many smaller, less heavily built breeds, but their bulk means they are unsuitable for many modern homes. If

toy dogs are not spoilt by their owners they make lively and amusing companions that can fit in anywhere and they are often very good watchdogs.

The gundog's role was to find game for the sportsman but to refrain from chasing it; in other words they had to be extremely obedient. Most gundogs are therefore amenable to discipline but they also have plenty of energy and stamina that needs to find an outlet. Terriers, mostly bred for vermin killing, tend to be tough, hardy, active and quick. They can be aggressive and also sometimes noisy and excitable.

Sheepdogs can be divided into two groups; those bred to work sheep and those bred to guard the flocks. The latter may have a strong guarding instinct that you will find necessary to control. The former are often the most sensitive and responsive of dogs, but they need something to exercise their minds as well as their bodies. Boredom can make them unreliable and neurotic. The Spitz breeds are usually bold, hardy, adaptable dogs with strong wills. One or two of the Spitz breeds tend to be rather noisy.

The basic dog shape is that of a medium-sized dingo type animal and the further it deviates from this norm, the more likely it becomes that the exaggeration of proportion represents a health risk to the dog. Giant breeds or those with large heads and very flattened muzzles tend to have a shorter life span than other breeds. Very long backs, heavily wrinkled faces, protruding or, alternatively, very small eyes,

miniature size – all these things can be weaknesses from the health point of view. Serious dog breeders are always well aware of both the strengths and the defects of their chosen breed and take both health and temperament into account when planning their breeding programme.

Try to look at some adults of a breed that attracts you before deciding to buy a puppy. Although it may be a slower process to find one, always buy direct from a dog breeder if you can. Puppies bought from pet shops, markets or dealers are less likely to be healthy for they have had a greatly increased chance of being exposed to infection and will also have suffered the stress of being moved from one environment to another. The dog magazines carry breeders' advertisements and all breeds have clubs or societies looking after their interests, the secretaries' names and addresses of which can be obtained from the Kennel Club. These breed clubs can advise you of your nearest breeder, although remember that this does not necessarily mean that they recommend that person. The responsibility of buying from a particular litter rests with you and the choice is yours alone.

Below: *This Rhodesian Ridgeback shows the remarkable reversal of hair growth along the spine which gives the breed its name. The dog's origin is uncertain.*

Right: *The tiny Pomeranian is quite happy to live in a very small area and is an excellent watchdog. It is one of the most popular of all toy breeds.*

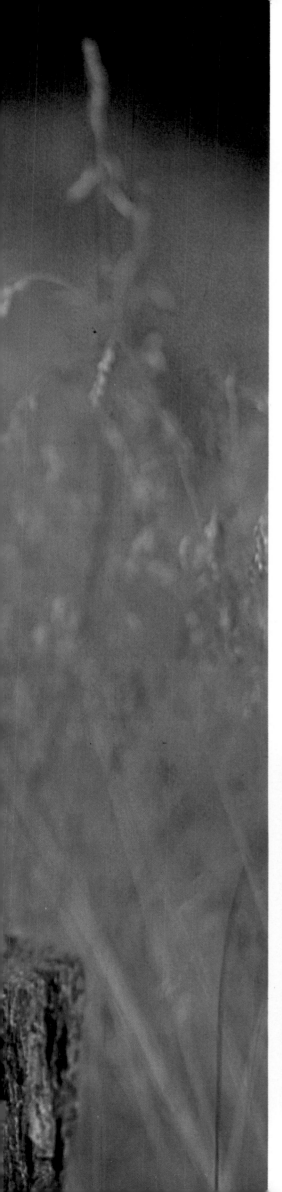

Puppyhood

Compared with the young of herbivores such as lambs and calves, puppies are born in a relatively undeveloped state. Whatever their breed, newly born puppies look very similar. All have their eyes closed and their ears folded and crumpled and they remain blind and deaf for almost the first three weeks of life. During this time they are responsive only to hunger, cold and pain. A new-born puppy's muzzle is short and blunt and its legs too small and weak to support the body weight, so that it can only crawl rather slowly. Whatever the adult coat is going to be like, the very young are covered with sleek short fur which may not necessarily be the colour of the coat in maturity.

There are differences in birth weights between breeds, of course, but these are not as great as might be expected. A puppy of a very small breed may weigh 100 g (4 oz) at birth and grow to a 2.7 kg (6 lb) adult, thus increasing its body weight 24 times. A giant breed might weigh 1 kg (2 lb) at birth and 45 kg (100 lb) when adult, an increase of 50 times in the body weight Proportionately, therefore, the large breeds have a lot more growing to do, and this is one of the reasons why they are slower to develop and mature. A tiny dog may be fully grown at nine months but a giant breed may not mature until two years old or more, and needs extra food for growth over a much longer period.

All mammals have a temperature-regulating mechanism which enables them to keep a constant body temperature even though the temperature of their surroundings may alter. This mechanism does not function in the newly born puppy, who can only keep warm by direct body contact with its mother. This is one of the reasons why a bitch will be very reluctant to leave a newly born litter for the first two or three days, knowing

Left: *Beagles are amongst the most popular of the hounds to keep as pets.*

Below: *These long-haired Dachshund puppies should prove to be good-natured and easy to train as they mature.*

as she does that their survival depends as much on her warmth as it does on the milk she is providing.

By about the tenth day of its life the puppy's eyes start to open, although at this stage it is still not able to focus or distinguish very much. As in kittens and most human babies the eyes are blue and gradually darken to the adult colour. It is not until about three weeks that puppies really start to respond to their environment. They are then able to see and hear, will start to get up on their feet and move rather unsteadily around, and the puppy or milk teeth are starting to erupt in the gums. At this stage weaning may be started with the very gradual introduction of solid food to supplement the bitch's milk. Given the chance puppies will now start to move away from their bed before relieving themselves. Previously defecation will have been stimulated by their mother's licking and the bitch herself cleaned up the nest.

Scientific research has established so-called 'critical' periods during the growth cycle of a number of animal species. If, during these periods, the young animal does not have the necessary environmental stimuli for its mental growth, it loses out in a way that cannot be rectified afterwards. Whatever was missing in the critical period cannot be replaced by later experience. From American research we know something about the critical periods in the development of a puppy. This is important since most people wanting a companion animal would like to end up with a confident, non-aggressive, friendly adult, and the treatment puppies receive during the critical periods can influence this. Such a character, however, is the product of both inherited characteristics and various environmental influences

We know that between the third and

the seventh week of a puppy's life it has a strong need both for its mother and its litter mates. During this period puppies learn by playing and by exploring their surroundings. The play, which is conducted with the litter mates and the mother, is necessary if the puppy is to develop the right relationship with its own species. Puppies that miss out on this early canine socialization may become aggressive, noisy and nervous, or difficult to breed as adults. From the fifth week onwards puppies need regular contact with humans if the man/dog relationship is to be successful. Puppies that have no human contact at all are virtually wild at three months old. Thereafter they are never able to form a close relationship with people and are very difficult to train in any way.

Puppies are usually sold at eight weeks old, by which time they are fully weaned. Modern research again suggests that between the seventh and eighth week is the best time for the puppy to change ownership. When you have decided on a breed, what should you look for when you go to choose a puppy from a litter? Good health and good temperament are of paramount importance in a companion animal, although the latter will depend as much on your handling of the puppy after you have bought it as on the way it has been treated to date.

There are a number of points that indicate puppies are healthy. They will have a well rounded appearance with no discharge from their eyes or nose. Their skin should be supple with no sores, bare patches or evidence of parasites. Puppies spend their time in

periods of activity alternating with periods of deep sleep; those that appear generally listless and uninterested may not be healthy. All the puppies in the litter, and their surroundings, should look clean. There should be enough space close to the nest for the puppies to play and also to satisfy their instinct to move away before relieving themselves, for this is the instinct you will be using when you begin to house-train your dog.

It will probably not be possible to see both parents of the puppies, but you should see the mother. Note whether she has the temperament characteristic of the breed and try to determine that she is neither nervous nor aggressive. Most breeders will prefer you to choose your puppy before the litter is ready to leave, and you may be asked to pay a non-returnable

booking fee which will be deducted from the purchase price when you collect your animal. Ask as many questions as you can when choosing a puppy, including when the litter was wormed and what exactly the puppies are being fed. Many breeders will provide you with a diet sheet; if you want to change the diet, try to do so gradually after the puppy has settled in with you.

When you collect your puppy you should receive a copy of the pedigree and hopefully also the registration papers. The latter are sometimes delayed by the Kennel Club and may have to be sent to you later. You should have prepared a bed for your puppy before bringing it home. A cardboard box of an appropriate size is ideal for a growing animal, since it can easily be discarded and replaced by a larger one as needed. Cut an entrance in the side for easy access and line the inside with some washable fabric as bedding. The most useful piece of equipment that you can have at this stage is a pen where the puppy can be confined for short periods when you cannot keep an eye on it.

Most puppies suffer from car-sickness, so take a towel and a roll of kitchen paper with you when collecting it. Travel sickness is mainly caused by stress so the less fuss you make about it the better. Dogs can usually be cured of travel sickness by

Above: *Both yellow and black Labrador Retrievers can quite often occur in the same litter.*

Right: *Colour changes in the coat are usual in some breeds as the dog matures. This Old English Sheepdog puppy will become grey and white.*

taking them for a daily short run in the car, especially if this ends in something pleasant such as a meal or a tit-bit. If you are really perturbed by the mess, then put the puppy in a newspaper-lined box for these short outings; your tensions will only aggravate the problem.

As soon as you get the puppy home, take it outside, for the first thing it will want to do is to produce a large puddle. If you have put it down in the right place before this happens, then you can praise it. If, however, it is the first thing it does once inside the house, then you can only blame yourself for lack of foresight. House-training is a matter of patience and observation. Puppies are still very much babies; they need to relieve themselves often and have little control over this function, so that they cannot wait until you are ready to let them out. When a puppy begins to sniff in circles, you should pick it up and take it outside. Stay with it so that you can praise the right action in the right place. Always take the puppy out immediately after it has had a meal or

A dog from the past

There, under the single arch of the South Bridge, is a huge mastiff, sauntering down the middle of the causeway, as if with his hands in his pockets; he is old, grey, brindled, as big as a little Highland bull, and has the Shakesperian dewlaps shaking as he goes . . .

There are no such dogs now. He belonged to a lost tribe. As I have said he was brindled, and grey like Rubislaw granite; his hair short, hard, and close, like a lion's; his body thickset, like a little bull – a sort of compressed Hercules of a dog. He must have been ninety pounds weight, at the least; he had a large blunt head; his muzzle black as night, his mouth blacker than any night, a tooth or two – being all he had – gleaming out of his jaws of darkness. His head was scarred with the records of old wounds, a sort of series of fields of battle all over it . . .

Rab had the dignity and simplicity of great size; and having fought his way all along the road to absolute supremacy, he was as mighty in his own line as Julius Caesar or the Duke of Wellington, and had the gravity of all great fighters.

Rab and His Friends
Dr John Brown
first published 1858

extra vitamins, and it is as harmful to feed too much as it is to give too little. If you are using food already containing balanced vitamins then add small quantities of bonemeal (*not* the horticultural variety) to the puppy's food; this will satisfy its requirements for extra calcium and phosphorus throughout growth.

A well-reared puppy will have been wormed for roundworms at least twice by the time it is eight weeks old. Unless you see signs of worm infestation it should not need worming again until it is about four months, and thereafter at yearly intervals. A puppy with worms may have a pot belly and a voracious appetite, and will pass worms in its faeces or, in severe cases, in vomit.

Below: *Puppies, like all babies, need small and frequent meals. Well reared puppies show a pleasantly rounded appearance and a natural inquisitiveness in what is going on around them. This is a litter of Cocker Spaniels.*

an energetic period of play, and remember that it is unlikely to be able to remain clean for more than about a couple of hours at this very early stage in its life. This is where a pen can be very useful during the periods when you cannot keep a constant watch. Lined with newspaper and with the puppy's bed and a toy inside it, the pen makes a safe place to leave the animal for short periods and even overnight.

Wire-mesh panelled, wooden framed pens specially constructed for puppies may be purchased at pet shops. Alternatively, you could improvize by using a child's play pen with wire mesh attached to the sides so that the puppy can not squeeze through the bars, or by making a pen using wire-mesh panels sold for various gardening activities.

Deprived of company for the first time in its life, a young puppy will very often cry and whine during the first few nights that it is on its own. A well-wrapped hot water bottle to snuggle up against may help. By all means comfort the puppy if it seems to be getting hysterical, but try to maintain a matter-of-fact approach. Obviously it is not fair to scold a very young animal that is making a fuss because it is alone for the first time in its life. On the other hand, you do not want to set up an association of ideas whereby the dog knows it has only to make a noise for some sympathetic person to appear. Most puppies will settle quite

happily into their new surroundings after a few days. In order to lay the foundations for having an adult dog that will remain quietly when left, it is wise to include a short period of about half an hour in the daily routine when the puppy is shut up alone during the day. Choose a period when it is already sleepy, but be firm about leaving it alone, even if it makes a fuss.

At eight weeks old, puppies should be having four meals a day – two meat and two milky cereal meals. As the animal grows, so of course the quantities need to be increased, but by three months the meals should be reduced to three in number, and by six months to two. Most adult dogs of a year or more are happy to have one main meal a day. It is impossible to give general advice about quantities to feed, as not only do breeds obviously differ very much in their requirements, but also individual animals differ quite widely in their food needs. Seek advice from a breed expert or dog breeder to establish guidelines to help you plan your puppy's diet.

Throughout their growth period, puppies need good food if they are to develop their potential. They will also benefit from a vitamin and mineral supplement to their diet. Your pet shop will be able to supply this, but if you are feeding with tinned or packaged food look at the list of ingredients on the label. Some manufacturers add

Roundworms look like yellowish pieces of string and can be up to 7.5–10 cm (3–4 ins) long. Worming tablets can be obtained from most chemists or your veterinary surgeon. As with all medicines, the correct dosage is very important, so follow the written directions carefully.

The earlier the puppy is introduced to the noisy world of traffic and crowds, the better chance it has of becoming a stable and confident adult. This advice cannot be followed, however, until the dog has been inoculated. All dogs need protection throughout their lives against a number of viral infections which are both common, and often lethal. This protection is given as an inoculation by a combined vaccine when they are puppies and maintained thereafter by booster inoculations at intervals (usually yearly) as advised by your veterinary surgeon. Inoculation protects puppies against distemper

and hardpad, viral hepatitis and leptospiral infections. Until inoculated, the puppy should not meet other dogs or walk on ground frequented by strange dogs. The development of all the vaccines has been an enormous boon to dog owners. Though no inoculation programme can ever be one hundred per cent successful, distemper, which used to be the scourge of many kennels, is now a rarity amongst well-cared-for dogs.

Although puppies of small breeds can quite conveniently be carried and all puppies can travel by car, it is much better for them to learn to cope with the unfamiliar situations and noises of the outside world as soon as possible. Some vaccination programmes dictate that the puppy cannot be taken out until it is three and a half months old, which means that some very formative weeks in the animal's life are wasted from the point of view of encountering new experiences. However, there are

vaccines that can be used earlier than three months and it is worth while discussing the whole subject with your veterinary surgeon.

Young puppies are learning from their surroundings the whole time, and the more they are able to explore and investigate, within reason, the better. The owner's role in these early stages is to encourage good habits and prevent bad habits from forming. Always look at your puppy's behaviour in the light of what you will want in an adult animal who may be part of the family for some years to come. If you do not want your dog on beds and chairs, then the struggles of a small puppy to get up into an armchair should be discouraged from the start, even if the spectacle is rather amusing. A puppy that growls in defence of a bone as large as itself may look funny, but should be dealt with sternly at the time. A too possessive adult dog from whom you cannot take a toy or a food

Left: *The West Highland White is full of cheeky charm. Dirt easily brushes out of the harsh coat which does, however, need trimming two or three times a year to keep it in good condition.*

Above: *The Jack Russell is a sporty little terrier, full of pep and self-confidence and renowned as a working dog.*

bowl is at best a nuisance and at worst a positive danger.

If your puppy shows reluctance in parting with a toy or bone when you give the command, take the animal gently, but firmly, by the scruff of the neck and remove the disputed object, saying 'Give'. If there are signs of resentment, give the puppy's head a little shake and say the word 'No' firmly. As soon as the puppy seems resigned to letting you have its prize, praise it and then give the object back. As with all training, this exercise must be repeated time and again until you have achieved the desired result – that is, an animal that will let you take anything away from it without a fuss.

The dog is a social being that in the wild would live in a pack, where acceptable behaviour is maintained by the pack leader's dominance over the other members. The family dog is also in a social situation which has its own disciplines. You are a substitute for the leader of the pack and your responsibility therefore is to encourage the dog to behave in an acceptable manner. To do this some

training of the puppy is necessary and this is easier if you follow some of the general principles used by all animal trainers. Dogs can only associate your behaviour with what they are doing at the time. To punish an animal for some past action is as ineffective as threatening future retribution for something it has not even thought of doing yet! A dog will tend to repeat an action which has a pleasant result and is less likely to repeat something that ended unpleasantly. Learning is a slow process in any animal, so repetition, patience and consistency on the part of the trainer are prime requirements.

During its growth, a puppy needs to play, explore and sleep. It cannot concentrate for any length of time, and too much should not be expected of it too early. On the other hand, the foundations should be laid for future obedience while it is still young.

The first thing a new puppy needs to know is its own name, which it should always associate with pleasure. Call the dog by name to feed it, give it a titbit, play with it or make a fuss of it. Never call it by name when correcting it for doing something of which you disapprove. In that situation always go to the dog and try to catch it in the act of misdemeanor. For example, if your dog is rolling in something obnoxious and you call it, when it comes to you, you must praise it. The animal will not connect your displeasure with its offensive odour,

27

but with the fact that it came to you in answer to its name.

A puppy should also be taught the meaning of the word 'No', which should be used forcefully but not shouted. Dogs are very sensitive to nuances of tone, and you can make use of this by the amount of enthusiasm or displeasure you show in your voice. Since a puppy cannot comprehend that 'No' means leave it alone, you must teach it by making sure that you are always in a position to enforce the word when you use it.

Collar and lead training should be started when the puppy is eight weeks old, even though you will not be able to take the dog out until it has been inoculated. A very young puppy will automatically want to follow you closely, as its instinct will be to stay with its mother or mother substitute. Unfortunately this delightful comradeship will not last, but you should make use of it while it does.

Buckle a lightweight collar comfortably round the puppy's neck and leave it there until it has become resigned to the fact that it cannot rid itself of this encumbrance by scratching. Then attach a lead to the collar and encourage the puppy to come with you by using a lot of cheerful persuasion. If this is done early enough, most struggles will be avoided. Always begin lead training a puppy in familiar surroundings, either around your garden or even in the house. When one sees a puppy being dragged reluctantly along the street, the reluctance is often caused by the puppy being frightened by a noise or by circumstances which are strange to it. Some puppies do take exception to a collar and lead, but they have to be taught to accept them. Really the only way to do this is by pulling the puppy along in short bursts for a few minutes a day, praising and encouraging it all the time. As the dog grows older,

correct any tendency to pull by a quick, firm jerk on the lead and the word 'No', followed by praise when the dog assumes its position by your side.

Puppies do not need formal exercise before about six months of age but, as already discussed, they do need to meet as many people, new situations and other dogs as possible. A puppy which shows fear of the unfamiliar should be encouraged to investigate it in a matter-of-fact manner. If you show too much sympathy in your tone and manner, you may be reinforcing the animal's suspicion that the situation is dangerous.

It is natural for puppies to chew and also to use their teeth in play. This is one of the reasons why they should have a number of toys that they can legitimately gnaw at and these should be of a kind that cannot be taken apart and swallowed. The only exception to this are the special dog toys made of cow hide, which does no harm if

swallowed. Large, uncooked bones provide all dogs with hours of enjoyment and help to keep teeth and gums healthy. Do not give them cooked bones which tend to splinter. Poultry, rabbit and fish bones are all especially dangerous, as they are extremely brittle.

At about four months old, the puppy teeth are pushed out by the growth of the adult set. Most puppies teethe without any trouble, though occasionally sore gums will put them off their food for a day or two. If a puppy does go off its food, make sure that it is its teeth that are the cause and that it is not actually sickening for something.

Puppies can be very rough when playing and as the puppy teeth are needle sharp, a nip or bite can be unpleasant for the owner. A bitch with a litter will growl a warning at a puppy that is biting too hard for her comfort and will then follow this with a snap if the puppy takes no notice. You, too, should prevent the puppy biting too hard by the use of the word 'No' followed by a small shake if it continues to ignore you.

Besides teaching your puppy to walk obediently by your side on a collar and lead and to answer to its name, there is one other very useful accomplishment that you can start teaching at about the age of four to five months. That is for it to lie down when you tell it to. As the dog gets older, you can build on this exercise until you have an animal that will drop flat on your command wherever it is, and will stay there until you tell it to move. The exercise can, in fact, be taught at any age, but it is easier to put a puppy in the right position on the ground than to struggle with a boisterous adult that does not understand what you are trying to achieve.

When you are teaching something new, always put the puppy on a lead so that you are in control, and always use the same word or action in connection with the particular exercise you are trying to teach. The word you use is immaterial, since all that you are attempting to do is to build an

Left: This colour of Rough Collie is called sable and white. The puppy coat lengthens as the dog matures.

Right: A Cavalier King Charles Spaniel bitch keeps a watchful eye open while her puppies sleep.

association in the dog's mind between a particular sound and a particular action. However, the word 'Flat' is probably preferable to 'Down' when teaching a dog to lie down, as the latter is liable to be used by other people should the puppy jump up at them, thereby leading to confusion. Give the command, push the puppy down into the right position and hold it there whilst praising it. Finally let it get up on your say so; 'O.K.' or 'All right' are good release words. Patient repetition at intervals of this procedure will finally result in the puppy lying down of its own accord when told. This is as far as you should go with this in a young puppy. Equally, do not be tempted to show off to other people by asking your puppy to lie down off the lead or in a place it has a choice of not obeying if it pleases. Taught slowly and carefully, this exercise can assist greatly towards having an adult dog that is always under your control, but

any attempt to rush the learning process is liable to end in unreliability and frequent disobediences throughout the dog's life.

When your dog is six months old, you will need to buy a licence for it. This can be obtained from any Post Office. From this age, too, all dogs kept in Britain must have a disc or tag giving the name and address of their owner attached to their collar. It is also the period that you can start taking your dog to a training club if you want to do so. These clubs have the advantage of trainers who are experienced in handling dogs of all types and can give advice on specific problems.

From six months to maturity (which varies from breed to breed), your dog may be likened to an adolescent who is anxious to try new experiences which may cause it to be not always as co-operative with authority as one would like!

The family dog

The dog is a highly adaptable animal in many ways and can flourish on a wide variety of diets, provided certain basic rules are observed. Dogs are carnivores – meat-eaters – so meat, or its protein equivalent, must form half to two thirds of the diet. Carbohydrates, in the form of cereal or biscuit, generally make up the rest of the meal, although some people like to add a small proportion of uncooked vegetable matter, such as raw carrot or greens. If the food is of good quality then the vitamins and minerals necessary to sustain life will already be present, and dietary supplements containing these are only necessary for the very young and old and for breeding bitches.

Left: *Dogs make the greatest companions for the young being always ready to join in with every pastime.*

Below: *Mongrel puppies can be a bit of a gamble when it comes to their looks and ultimate size.*

Fresh meat can be raw or cooked and a proportion of fat is beneficial. Meat can be replaced occasionally by fish (either filleted or pressure-cooked until the bones are soft and crumbly), cheese or eggs. Tinned dog meat, produced by a reputable manufacturer, is perfectly acceptable but check the label to see whether cereal has been added. Frozen meat must be thoroughly thawed. Commercially prepared, semi-moist foods in plastic packets are usually relished by dogs and have the advantage that, unopened, they will keep for a reasonable period; check the label to ascertain this. Dry foods, which provide a complete diet, are marketed in pellet form. These are the ultimate in convenience foods for they provide every nutritional need. All you have to do is to make sure that fresh water is always available. A dog should always have access to fresh water, but dried, complete foods, where all the water has been

Make sure that the ball is of a suitable size though, so that there is no danger of it getting wedged in the dog's gullet and choking it.

Grooming should also be part of the regular routine for a number of reasons. It will enable you to spot parasites or skin complaints before they have a chance to spread. Properly done, it massages the skin and tones up the muscles, helping maintain the dog in good health and giving it pleasure. Provided you keep the equipment clean, regular grooming means that you should have to bathe the dog very infrequently.

The procedure for grooming and how to do it varies from breed to breed, depending generally on whether you have a long- or short-haired dog. The subject of grooming is dealt with in more detail under the various breeds discussed in Top Dogs and this should help you in grooming your dog. A general point that may be made is that providing your dog is of a suitable size, it is much easier to groom it on a table than on the floor. The table should have a non-slip surface, and the first step towards trouble-free grooming is to teach your puppy to stand and lie down on this table without moving until you tell it that it may. Your aim is to have a dog that will lie happily relaxed on its side, and this can only be achieved by gentle persuasion and daily practice.

Mats and tangles on long-coated dogs occur most frequently behind the ears (where the coat is usually softer), behind the elbows and inside the thighs. If you do find any, first wedge the comb between the hair and the dog's skin in order to avoid nicking the skin. Then cut the tangle across with thinning scissors and tease the

extracted, will make the dog thirstier than other diets, so constant provision of water is even more important.

The carbohydrate in the diet can be supplemented by adding table scraps if desired. Biscuit meal added to the meat is the conventional way of adding carbohydrates, but large dog biscuits are better for the animal's teeth.

Dogs are very much creatures of habit so any change of diet should be introduced gradually over a period of time. Some very valuable foods, such as offal and milk, have a laxative effect on most dogs so do not give them too much of these items.

General advice about the quantity to feed a dog is impossible to give. Just like people, some dogs are good food converters, whilst others are not. Some of the very lively toy breeds and the small energetic terriers will need more food in proportion to their body weight than larger, more lethargic

dogs. To give some examples, a working German Shepherd, such as a police dog, may receive 750 g (1½ lbs) of meat and the same quantity of biscuit daily. A similar animal leading the more sedentary life of a pet would probably find about half this quantity sufficient, whilst a bitch of similar size nursing six three-week-old puppies, will need practically unlimited food – certainly at least three times the quantities mentioned and possibly even more.

Routine daily care of the dog should, if possible, be the responsibility of one person of the household. Few adult dogs ever get too much exercise and the minimum requirements listed under breeds are not only a daily necessity for the dog, but also invaluable for the owner's health. Playing ball games with your dog or teaching it to jump are both excellent ways of working off surplus energy.

Above left: *To chase and bring back a ball is almost instinctive in gundogs like this Spaniel puppy. Playing games with your dog is an excellent way of exercising it. By teaching the dog to bring back an article to you, you will be laying the foundations for an obedient pet, likely to respond to further training.*

Right: *The show Yorkshire Terrier has a long silky coat which reaches the ground. To prevent the coat breaking or getting matted, tresses of hair are rolled up in tissue paper which is held secure with a rubber band. Gentle brushing leaves a silky curtain of hair. Show Yorkies soon get used to this long grooming procedure and seem to enjoy all the fuss and attention that it entails.*

remnants out with your fingers. If you want to bathe the dog, the coat must be combed free of knots first or you will end up with even more. Only long-haired dogs will need combing. Various dog combs are sold; the best type to use is that made of steel, with teeth set fairly wide apart rather than those that are very fine.

It is of course possible to clip out a badly matted coat, but this tends to alter the texture of the hair. Incidentally, it is not necessary to clip a dog to keep it cool in summer.

Bathing should be done in luke-warm water using a dog or a human shampoo – never detergents or carbolic soaps. Rinsing must be very thorough and a spray is very helpful here. Drying is more important still. By using a shampoo you will have removed some of the oil in the coat that normally insulates the skin against wet and cold, and for this reason it is essential that the dog is completely dry before it goes outside.

Dogs fed correctly rarely develop dental trouble. Tartar may develop as a brown deposit, particularly at the base of the canine teeth. It can be scraped off with a dental scraper or the milled edge of a coin.

Right: *Each breed has its own grooming requirements. Here a Dandie Dinmont has its topknot combed upwards to give it its 'woolly' appearance.*

Below: *A dog should be combed thoroughly before bathing in lukewarm water, Apply shampoo to the head last of all and rub it in well. Rinsing must completely remove all the shampoo and is best done with a spray; otherwise several changes of water are necessary. Squeeze the surplus water from the coat before drying thoroughly with a towel. Keep the dog indoors for several hours after a bath as many like to roll as soon as they can.*

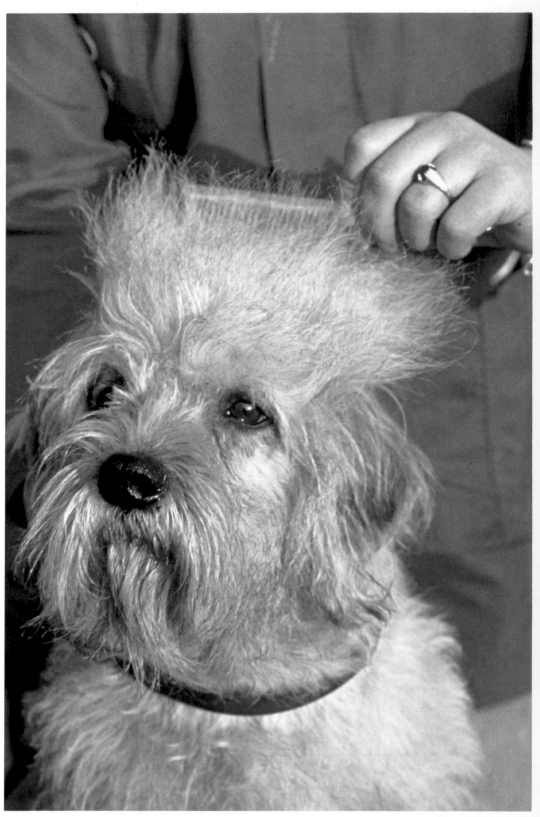

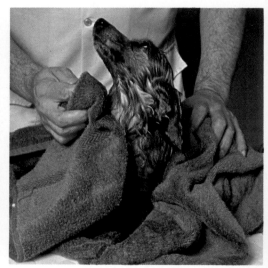

Right: *Nail clipping should not be needed very often if the dog is given enough exercise on hard surfaces. When it does have to be done, special clippers and great care must be used. The nails must not be cut too short.*

Well-exercised dogs should not need their claws cutting, since they will wear down naturally. However in an older dog these sometimes become overgrown and will then need trimming with nail clippers. Care must be taken when doing this, as there is a living quick of nerves and blood running down the centre of each nail. Cutting this will cause pain, so only remove the tip of each claw. Unfortunately trimming seems to stimulate growth and once it has been started you will have to make it a regular occurrence. Many breeds have dew claws, at least on their front legs. This is a fifth claw situated a little way up from the foot on the inside of the leg. The normal growth of a dew claw involves the shedding or breaking off of the tip at regular intervals, but it is wise to check that this is happening and that the claw is not becoming somewhat overgrown.

The dog has two scent glands on either side of the anus. The passage of the faeces is normally sufficient to empty these anal glands, but occasionally they become overfull, making the dog uncomfortable. It may then nibble its rear or rub its bottom along the ground. This trouble can be easily rectified by applying pressure in the right place; ask your veterinary surgeon to show you how to do this.

The commonest external parasite on the dog is the flea, and all dogs have fleas at some time in their lives. The dog flea does not live on humans, although it is not above biting them to see if they are a suitable host! Fleas may be suspected if your dog scratches, and confirmed by finding a small, swiftly moving brown insect, or a number of black specks, flea droppings, in the dog's coat. Insect powder rubbed well into the coat and brushed out, insecticidal shampoos or sprays are three ways of dealing with the problem. Alternatively, you can use a flea collar (a plastic band impregnated with insecticide), which will keep the dog free of external parasites for up to three months. These are effective but expensive, and look unsightly on short-coated dogs.

Lice are also parasitical on dogs, although they are encountered less frequently. They look like smooth grey blobs attached to the skin. Their hold must be loosened by a dab of methylated spirits before pulling them off, otherwise their heads remain embedded in the dog's skin. At certain times of the year your dog may pick up harvest mites, which cause intense irritation. If you notice the dog biting its feet frenziedly, especially if it has been through a recently harvested field, search between the toes for very small red specks. These are the mites in question. A weak solution of a suitable disinfectant will get rid of them, and this should be followed by an application of calamine lotion to the inflamed area.

The only two internal parasites which are met with at all frequently in the dog are roundworms (which mainly affect puppies) and tapeworms (which mainly affect adult animals). It should be emphasized that most parasites are specific to their host; in other words they cannot live in other animal species. Roundworms in both the dog and cat present a slight risk to human health in that if the roundworm eggs, which are passed in the faeces of infected animals, are swallowed, a larval cyst might possibly develop in the human body. The risk applies mainly to small children, when crawling or playing in gardens or parks where infected dogs have been present. Obviously such a risk would not occur in hygienic conditions and can be removed entirely by keeping your pet, whether cat or dog, worm free.

Tapeworms can weaken their canine host. Drugs prescribed by a veterinary surgeon should be administered and the dog should also be treated for fleas and lice, which can carry tapeworms to the dog. Tapeworm segments, resembling grains of rice or small maggots, are passed in the faeces of infected animals. These present no health risk to humans at any stage.

The diagnosis and treatment of sickness in a dog is the job of a veterinary surgeon and his chances of success are much improved if you take the animal to him as soon as it shows signs of ill health. Any unusual behaviour should be watched carefully. Symptoms that all is not well include such things as an energetic dog becoming listless, a greedy dog refusing food, excessive thirst, and a dog that shakes its head a lot or rubs it on the ground. Constant vomiting and diarrhoea need urgent attention, although diarrhoea on its own may be due to a change of diet. Starving the dog for twenty-four hours to see if the condition improves will do no harm at all to the animal.

Dogs in pain will bite, so a dog involved in an accident should have an improvised muzzle put on before any other action is taken. Any strip of material, such as a tie or a scarf, can be used. Make a loop in the middle of the strip and slip this over the dog's muzzle. Then knot it under the chin and tie the ends of the material at the back of the dog's neck.

Any bleeding should be staunched with a pad of clean material held firmly on the injury and the dog should be taken on an improvised stretcher as quickly as possible to a veterinary surgeon.

As with humans, the body temperature is the best indication of health or sickness. The normal temperature of a dog is 101.5°F, and more than a degree above or below this should be cause for concern. The dog's temperature is taken in the rectum and is more easily done if someone else holds the dog. Use a blunt-ended thermometer and lightly grease the bulb. Insert about 2.5 cm (1 in) of the thermometer into the anus with a slight twist and hold it in place for two minutes before withdrawing it and reading the result.

If your dog is unwell, your veterinary surgeon may prescribe drugs in liquid, capsule or powder form. Do not attempt to incorporate any of them into the dog's food, since it may leave some and you will then not know how much, if any, of the dose has been taken. Liquid doses are most easily given from a small bottle. Tell the dog to sit, then hold its head up with the mouth closed. Pull the corner of the lips out to form a pouch and trickle in the liquid slowly. As it reaches the back of the throat, the dog will automatically swallow. Powders can be shaken onto the back of the tongue and to open a dog's mouth in order to do this, gently press the lips against the teeth and gums.

Pills or capsules can be given in one of two ways and it is always worth trying the easier way first! Take three or four small pieces of butter and hide the pill in one of them. Feed these rapidly to the dog starting and finishing with an undoctored one. It is easy to spot if the pill is rejected, but most dogs with their eye on a further titbit will not even notice its presence. If this fails to work, however, you must open the dog's mouth and push the pill as far to the back as possible. Then hold the mouth shut and gently stroke the throat until you feel the dog swallow. Keep watch for a minute or two to make sure that the pill has gone, as some animals become very clever at holding things in their mouths to spit out later when you are not watching.

The average life-span of a dog varies from breed to breed. The giant breeds are very old at ten years, whilst a small active terrier may still be quite sprightly for another two or three years after this. Old dogs need warmth and quiet, and a bed large enough for them to stretch out on their side, as their joints may be too stiff to allow them to curl up comfortably. Good food, perhaps divided into two smaller meals instead of one large one, is another necessity. Old dogs tend to smell more than younger ones and veterinary chlorophyll tablets can help here. If at all possible, always let an old dog take life at its own pace, and remember that a dog whose eyesight is failing will still be quite happy in familiar surroundings, as scent will have played a much larger part in its life than sight. Finally, however sad the decision, do not prolong the life of a dog when it is so old that it no longer enjoys living. A veterinary surgeon can end suffering with a painless injection, and if you have loved and valued the animal as a friend, this is the last kindness that you can offer.

There is no magic way of training a dog, and methods which will work with one animal may fail with another. Some of the advice given on the common problems discussed may seem obvious, but people in the midst of a worrying or distressing situation do not always think as clearly as at other times. All the training methods

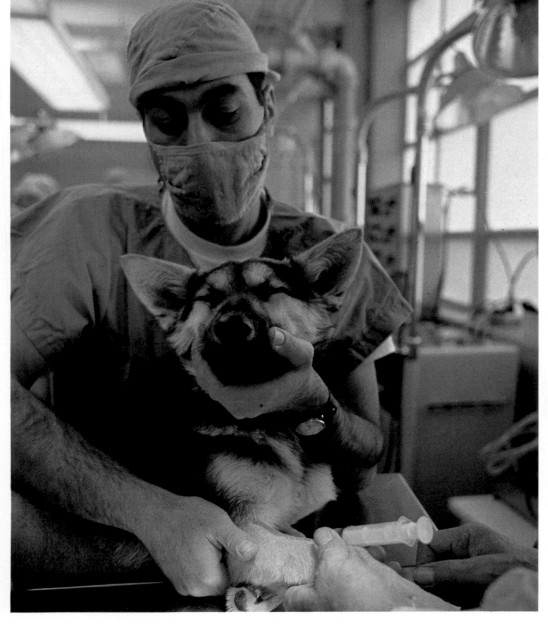

Left: *All dogs will occasionally need the expert attention of a veterinary surgeon to ensure continued good health.*

Right: *The Maremma is an Italian sheepdog with a very strong guarding instinct. It needs careful training.*

King George's Dalmatian. AD 1822

Yellow wheels and red wheels, wheels that squeak and roar,
Big buttons, brown wigs, and many capes of buff . . .
Someone's bound for Sussex in a coach-and-four;
And, when the long whips crack,
Running at the back
Barks the swift Dalmatian
Whose spots are seven score.

White dust and grey dust, fleeting tree and tower,
Brass horns and copper horns blowing loud and bluff,
Someone's bound for Sussex at eleven miles an hour;
And, when the long horns blow,
From the dust below
Barks the swift Dalmatian,
Tongued like an apple-flower.

Big domes and little domes, donkey-carts that jog,
High stocks and low pumps and incomparable snuff,
Someone strolls at Brighton, not very much incog.;
And, panting on the grass,
In his collar bossed with brass,
Lies the swift Dalmatian,
The King's plum-pudding dog.

Dorothy Margaret Stuart.

described are well tried and, if applied correctly, will work with most dogs, but always remember that you can get expert advice from your local training club if you feel you need it.

The dog that pulls on the lead, making life uncomfortable for itself and its owner, needs training on a slip collar. This type of collar needs to be put on and used correctly if it is to be effective. It should never be left on a loose dog, nor should an animal be tied up when wearing one, as there is a danger of it choking. Basically the collar is a length of chain with an equal sized ring at each end. To put it on correctly, hold a ring in one hand and let the chain slip through, then slip this loop over the dog's head. The loop has one sliding ring and one fixed ring. Your aim is to keep the dog level with you as you walk along and the collar is put on correctly when, with the dog in this position, the sliding ring is on the end of the chain coming under the dog's neck. This means that when the dog is not pulling the weight of the chain will keep the loop slack. Attach a leather or nylon lead with a trigger hook to the sliding ring of the slip collar. Do not use a chain lead as this is too uncomfortable to hold and can also be dangerous as it can severely cut into your hand.

Left: *The more you teach your dog, the more pleasure both of you will get from your relationship.*

Start walking with the dog on your left side and each time it attempts to forge ahead of you, give a short, sharp jerk on the lead to bring it back into the correct position. When the correct position is achieved, both lead and collar should be slack and your praise will encourage the dog to stay with you in this place. Using the collar in this way is effective if you are determined and consistent, and providing the relative weights and strengths of you and your dog give you sufficient advantage to jerk hard enough to make it uncomfortable for the animal. If, however, you are not strong enough to do this, try carrying a rolled newspaper in your right hand and tap the dog on the nose with it every time it attempts to pass you. This is not so satisfactory a method, as any sensible dog will attempt to go wide in an effort to get ahead, but you can correct that tendency by practising alongside a wall or fence.

Training a dog to walk on the left side of a person developed from the training given to police dogs. Leading the dog on the left side meant the leader's right hand was free, generally to hold a weapon. Nowadays, it has become accepted as a convention and as most people are right-handed, it is more convenient to keep the right hand free to open doors and so on.

Keep all training sessions short; practise regularly and remember that your praise for the right action is as

necessary as your correction for the wrong one at all times.

The dog that will not come when it is called may be the wilful type, or this may be the result of wrong handling on your part. Consider whether you have ever shouted at the dog when it returned to you after some misdemeanour. Such behaviour will make the animal shy of coming back. The best method of teaching a disobedient dog to come is to attach a light, strong line to its collar (use a leather collar, not a slip collar, in this instance). The line should be about 6 metres (20 feet) long and should be left trailing when you let the dog off its ordinary short lead. You should stand near the end of the line when you call the dog. Then if you get no response, jerk the line hard and call again. Any movement the dog makes towards you should be encouraged and when it reaches you, even if you have had to jerk it much of the way, you must be enthusiastic in your welcome before letting it go again. You may need to keep using the line for a number of weeks, depending on your skill, but do not be tempted to take it off too early. Remember that you are trying to build up a good habit by making sure the dog never has the chance to disobey the command you give.

The dog that roams cannot be cured, but it must be prevented. The habit develops either because the dog is turned out on its own by irresponsible

someone else driving, so that you are able to make sure the dog stays flat when the car is moving.

A dog that becomes hysterical in a car, barking at anything that moves outside should be tied up low down on the floor of the vehicle so that it cannot see out of the windows. Noisy dogs cause a great deal of bad feeling, as well as being a potential danger.

The command to lie down instantly can also be used with a dog that will not come when called. In such a case, you may be able to make it drop to the ground and then go up to it.

Some breeds bark considerably more

Left: A dog guard across the open tailgate of an estate car ensures that the dogs inside get enough air when they do have to be left in this situation.

Below: Labrador Retrievers love water and are strong swimmers.

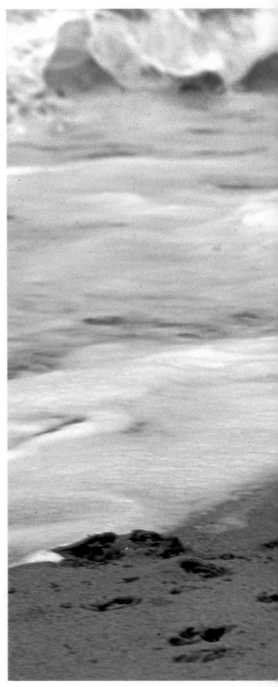

owners or because the outside world provides more attractions than home or owner. Adequate fencing or kennelling are both solutions if you cannot rely on people to keep the right doors shut. If you feel that you are going to have to chain your dog up for part of the day, then try to tether it on a running line rather than from a fixed point. Fix a wire to a post, making sure there is another one close by, similar to those positioned for a clothes line. Pass the wire through the end link of a light chain and fasten the other end of the wire to the second post. Clip the chain to the dog's collar. The chain must have at least one swivel link so that the dog cannot get tangled up and it must be long enough for the dog to be able to lie down in a weatherproof kennel, which should be placed by one of the posts. The dog thus has the freedom of a strip of ground, and little danger of becoming entangled in the chain. Such confinement is preferable to the dangers of a dog running wild, but must be used with discretion and balanced with giving the dog adequate exercise and periods of controlled freedom. If you do not do this, you will have a bored animal who may become both noisy and aggressive.

Destructive dogs usually become so through boredom or jealousy, and is, in fact, one of the few bad habits which most dogs outgrow. However, a young energetic dog shut up for long periods on its own will take out its frustration on its surroundings. Your anger at

finding devastation on your return is not going to be effective, since it is very unlikely that the dog will associate the correction with the things it was busy tearing up an hour previously. Since the dog must obviously be left on its own on occasions, it is only sensible to leave it where it cannot do harm. If kennelling in a draught-free garage or outhouse is not possible, you should consider buying a wire crate. This is a fairly costly item, as it must be big enough for the dog to stand up and turn round in easily, but it may be cheaper to buy one in the long run than to restore the damage done otherwise. No dog should be crated for more than two or three hours at a time unless absolutely necessary, such as it going on a long journey. Try always to leave the dog with something it can acceptably use its teeth on such as a rawhide toy or a large, uncooked bone. This will help to relieve boredom.

Dogs that are excitable car travellers are both a nuisance and a potential danger. If you have taught your puppy to lie down on command, continue this training until you have a dog that will lie down when and wherever you tell it, remaining there until you let it move.

When the dog is reliable at staying in one position, make him maintain it in the car, while it is stationary and the doors are open. Make sure the dog is lying in the place where you want him to stay during a journey. Finally attempt some short journeys with than others and this is something to be borne in mind when choosing a dog. Most dogs that bark consistently do so because they are bored or lonely. Without removing the cause, you cannot expect to effect a cure. One of the easiest ways to teach a dog to stop barking on command is to say 'Quiet' and to hold its mouth shut. As with all training, though, this has to be repeated again and again with the same command and suitable praise. Only when you are perfectly satisfied that the dog understands what is wanted are you justified in correcting it if it ignores you.

Highly trained guard dogs need highly trained handlers, but many ordinary people keep a dog as some form of protection and guard. In doing this, you may run into two problems; your dog may be too protective and not allow the tradesmen to get to the front door, or, if you acquired it as an adult, it may greet everyone as a friend. In both cases, if the dog is inside when the door bell rings make it lie down a little way back from the door, but where it can see and be seen. When you open the door, the aggressive dog is therefore under your control and, from the point of view of the caller on the doorstep, the over-friendly dog in the background is an unknown quantity, which is generally sufficient deterrent in itself. If you make this a regular habit every time you answer the door, you will find that the dog will anticipate your command and take up the right position when it hears the bell. Guard against becoming careless, though, and letting the dog get up before you say it may.

Even the most highly trained working dogs need refresher training courses from time to time, so do not be afraid to go right back to square one with a dog which knew something at one time but appears to have forgotten the meaning of a command later.

Dogs, just like people, are individuals with varying amounts of initiative which they will use to their own advantage. Hopefully, if you have brought up your puppy sensibly, you will produce a well-behaved adult animal. Problems can occur, however, and since bad habits only tend to get worse, you should always seek some sort of ready solution. By training your dog you cannot alter its essential nature, but you can control undesirable behaviour. You will need patience and persistence and, above all, a strong desire to succeed. Many unruly dogs, having sized up a weak-willed owner, continue to take advantage of the situation and repeatedly get their own way.

Top dogs

The Yorkshire Terrier
This is one of the top favourites amongst the toy breeds and makes a good choice of pet for anyone who lives in a restricted space or who finds long walks difficult. The charm of the breed lies in its courage and self-importance – typical terrier attributes, but somehow particularly appealing in a dog so small. This spirited character carries a magnificent coat of dark steel blue and tan, which in the show dog sweeps the floor like a silky curtain.

The breed is not very old compared to some, having been developed mainly in the mining areas of Yorkshire during the latter half of the nineteenth century. It is not known just how the breed originated, but it is thought that various small ratting terriers were used in its development, which would account for the breed's gameness and also for the sound, workmanlike shape of the dog under its voluminous coat.

In the early days, these dogs varied greatly in size, some weighing as much as 4.5 kg (10 lbs) and some as little as 1 kg (2 lbs). They also fetched very good prices, which doubtless encouraged many a miner's wife to rear litters of puppies in the hope of selling them at a profit to show fanciers. Such rearing conditions probably account for the sociable, affectionate nature of the Yorkie as we know it today.

The modern Yorkshire Terrier should not weigh more than 3 kg (7 lbs) and most show dogs weigh much less. However, the breed still has not stabilized completely in size. A percentage of oversize puppies are still born, and are often sold comparatively cheaply. These are often a better buy for the average owner as they are less liable to accidental injury than the

Left: *The black and gold markings on this German Shepherd are one of the most popular colour combinations in this breed. The density and thickness of its coat effectively protect the dog in unfavourable weather conditions.*

Below: *Yorkshire Terriers vary in size, the larger animals often making better pets as they are hardier and stronger.*

really tiny mites, and although still small enough (even as adults) to be tucked under one arm, they are also big enough to enjoy the pleasures of exploring on a country walk. Very small dogs are not really suitable companions for young children who tend to regard them as playthings rather than playmates. Being accidentally dropped or handled a little too roughly can seriously frighten or even injure a toy puppy, whereas a youngster of a larger and sturdier breed is more able to take such rough and tumble in its stride.

Yorkie puppies are black and tan in colour, but the black puppy coat changes to dark steel blue as the dog matures. Grooming the adult show dog is a specialised business, although exactly the same equipment is needed for the pet animal. This consists of a soft, springy bristle brush, a metal comb with rounded ends to the teeth and a pair of small blunt-nosed scissors. Accustom the puppy to gentle daily grooming. Start by laying him on his back in your lap whilst you brush the inner thighs, the lower part of the chest and the front legs. Then stand the dog on all fours and gently brush

the fur up on the body and finally down from the parting along the spine. This daily routine will quickly be accepted by the dog as a pleasurable procedure, and ensures that no tangles develop.

It may be necessary to trim the hair from the top of the Yorkie puppy's ears to encourage them to stand erect, and also to trim the hair between the toes and round the edges of the feet if it gets very long. As the hair on the head grows longer, the topknot can be either tied up with a ribbon to keep the hair out of the dog's eyes or, in the pet dog, can be cut in a fringe. It may also be necessary to trim some of the hair under the tail. A pet living an active life will not grow so long a coat as the show dog. Many pet Yorkies have their coat trimmed about 10 cm (4 ins) from the ground level, as this makes them easier to look after and prevents them from getting too muddy and wet. A good human shampoo, preferably based on almond or olive oil, is suitable for bathing and the coat should be patted and squeezed dry (not rubbed) with warm towels before brushing away the final dampness.

Very tiny puppy collars are difficult to find, but do not use a cat collar as

these are very often elasticated and a puppy can wriggle out of them in moments of excitement or danger. A watch-strap will often make a suitable collar for a Yorkie puppy, at least until it grows larger. Small dogs can get through even smaller spaces than might seem possible, so fencing must be extra secure. Flat dwellers without a garden can train toy dogs to use newspaper-lined trays for toilet purposes. If you have to use this method you must also encourage your dog to relieve itself when out for a walk, or you may find that you have a dog which requires a newspaper every time. Finally, remember that small dogs are very appealing and very easy to steal, so do not leave your pet where it could be taken.

Below: *The show Yorkshire Terrier has a dark steel blue coat which sweeps the ground. The tan markings should be rich and bright.*

Right: *The Standard is the largest of the three varieties of Poodle. They are always self-coloured, i.e. the same colour all over. This is a brown whose entire coat has been clipped evenly. If left unclipped, the coat of a Poodle grows thick and either fluffy or curly.*

The Poodle

The name 'Poodle' comes from the German word 'pudel', meaning to splash in water, and this suggests that the dog's origin might be German rather than French, as popularly supposed. However, the breed was so well known in the past across wide areas of Europe that the exact country of origin is likely to remain speculative. The breed was first known as a sporting dog, whose fondness for water and aptitude for swimming made it an excellent retriever of wildfowl. The similarity between Poodles and Water Spaniels is apparent today and it is possible that they share a common ancestor from previous times.

The vivacity of the Poodle and the readiness with which it could be taught tricks made it a favourite with showmen very early in history. Travelling bands of entertainers with jugglers, dancing bears and performing dogs were familiar figures as far north as Russia and as far south as Italy. These dogs were often shaved or clipped in a fantastic way and the barbering of a Poodle's coat became quite a lucrative trade, reaching its zenith in the late nineteenth century.

At this time fashionable Poodles in Paris and London were clipped to show their owner's armorial crests, or symbols of good luck, or to carry messages of love. At about the same date, corded Poodles were exhibited, the hair on the unclipped portion of the dog being allowed to grow as long as possible before being twisted into ringlets, which were kept oiled to prevent them breaking off. One of the most famous of these dogs was said to be 60 cm (2 ft) high at the shoulder and to have cords 90 cm (3 ft) long. These of course had to be tied up when the animal was not being exhibited to prevent it tripping over its own hair.

The modern Poodle comes in three sizes.

The Standard Poodle is the oldest variety and is usually a sensible dog with an excellent temperament. It is, however, the least popular, possibly because it is a large dog needing a lot of food, exercise and coat care. Miniatures were developed at the beginning of the twentieth century by breeding down from the standard size. They were very popular until eclipsed by the Toy Poodle, which was not officially recognized by the Kennel

Above: *This apricot Toy Poodle is just coming up to the age when it will need its first puppy clip. This diminutive dog is very popular among the toy breeds.*

Right: *This white Standard Poodle is in the full magnificence of a lion clip while her young litter still display the curly charms of the soft puppy coat.*

Club until the 1950s. There is no reason why the Toy Poodle should be particularly delicate, but some can be faddy and neurotic, so be careful to choose a sturdy, friendly puppy if you want this size.

All Poodles have a real zest for life. They are intelligent and have a great sense of fun, which is why they are so popular. The oldest coat colours appear to have been brown, white and black, but there are now a wide range of solid colours from which to choose, including cream, apricot, silver and blue. Poodle puppies are not necessarily born the colour they will become as adults. Silver and blue Poodles, for example, are born black. Those very familiar with the breed will tell you that differences of temperament are associated with the different colours of coat, a

trimmed) up to the age of a year and then have to be shown in either Lion or Continental clip.

The Lion clip is most generally used on show Poodles in Great Britain. The face and the body of the dog are shaved, leaving a luxurious mane of hair over the shoulders and part of the rib cage. The hair is shaved off the front legs leaving bracelets of hair around the wrists, and off the hind legs leaving two bracelets of hair on each leg. A pom-pon of hair is left on the end of the tail. The Continental clip is similar to the Lion, but leaves patterns of hair on the hindquarters.

The narrow, hair-filled ear canals, which do not allow the air to circulate, make Poodles rather prone to ear troubles. To avoid these, try to keep the inside of the ear free from hair. Dust the ear with a little boracic powder and, taking two or three hairs between your finger and thumb, jerk them out quickly. This should not distress the dog at all unless you try to remove too many hairs at once or unless the ear is already sore. Examine the inside of the ear flaps each week, and, if necessary, clean them with damp cotton wool and dust occasionally with boracic powder. Signs of ear trouble include the dog shaking its head, the ear feeling hot and tender to the touch, an evil-smelling discharge or a lot of brown, sticky wax. Such conditions should receive veterinary attention without delay as they can become chronic if neglected.

The German Shepherd Dog (Alsatian)

This breed may be regarded as the premier working dog of the world, for it is versatile and adaptable enough to do almost any job that a dog may be required to do. It is also widely kept as a companion and, with responsible ownership, can be one of the most satisfying breeds to own.

Compared with some, this is not a very old breed. The credit for the temperamental and physical characteristics which make it outstanding must go to the German

Above left: *The trainability, physique and intelligence of German Shepherds make them ideal for the work of finding avalanche victims.*

Right: *Clearing a long jump on command is just one part of the extensive training of a police dog.*

phenomenon not unknown in other breeds which display distinct colour varieties.

The Poodle does not shed hair but the coat, which is harsh, profuse and naturally curly, does mat and tangle and needs regular daily grooming. The grooming equipment needed includes a wire brush, a coarse-toothed metal comb and scissors. Part the hair along the middle of the stomach and start brushing it upwards in layers towards the middle of the back. Each of these layers should be small, so that the brushing gets down to the skin. Next, brush the two legs that are uppermost, being careful to include the inner thighs and armpits where mats form easily. Turn the dog over and repeat the process. Then sit the animal facing you, and brush the chest and neck in layers upwards. Finish with the top-

knot, ears and tail. Toy dogs are often small enough for all this to be done as they lie on your lap.

The adult Poodle will need its coat clipping and bathing every six or eight weeks, and it is usual for the dog to go to a beauty parlour for this to be done. You can do it yourself if you know how, but it does involve buying a number of expensive items of equipment including electric clippers, some form of spray for rinsing and a dog hair dryer (human ones are not really powerful enough). Puppies need to have only their feet and tail trimmed, and this should be done at about four months. There are a multitude of different pet trims or clips for you to choose from, all aimed at keeping the coat within manageable proportions. Show dogs are kept in a puppy clip (i.e. just their feet and tail

fanciers who established the German Shepherd as we know it today some eighty or ninety years ago. Sheepdogs from the areas of Wurtemburg and Thuringia provided the basis for the breed. These animals were used not only to protect sheep but also to prevent the flocks straying from the pasture onto the unfenced arable land. Thus they had to be constantly watchful, virtually tireless and able to act on their own initiative. The present-day success of the German Shepherd owes much to the retention of these very qualities in the breed.

German dog breeders have always recognized that temperament is of equal importance to conformation in a working dog and the factors which make the German Shepherd so formidable are its alertness, reliability and power of concentration. There are other breeds that are tougher and faster or possess better scenting powers, but the willingness and determination of the German Shepherd dogs have made them widely popular with many organizations which need to use reliable trained dogs in quantity. German Shepherds were scarcely known outside their native land before the First World War, but both the German police and army appreciated their worth and they were used on the battlefields as messengers and also as rescue dogs to find the wounded. This brought them to the attention of United States and British soldiers, who took specimens home to both countries. In Britain it was felt

that any title containing the word German would be prejudicial to the breed's interests and they were renamed Alsatians, although the rest of the world still continued to use their original name. In 1977 the English Kennel Club decided that the original and descriptive name German Shepherd Dog should once again become their official title.

In the 1920s the German Shepherd enjoyed a phenomenal rise in popularity. Unfortunately, this resulted in more and more dogs being bred from inferior stock and many getting into inexperienced ownership. In consequence, mismanaged and temperamentally unsound animals brought the breed into disrepute and their numbers declined. That trend was once again reversed by the Second World War, when demand for working dogs of proven ability increased the numbers being bred.

The dog is strong and agile, with an effortless, springy gait which enables it to cover the maximum ground with the minimum exertion. Theoretically the coat can be any colour, although white is frowned upon; in practice the majority of German Shepherds have a black saddle with lighter markings of tan ranging through to cream. The black hair on a puppy will tend to decrease as the dog gets older and the other markings will spread and brighten. Fawn or golden puppies have coats that will darken and are called sables, and occasionally one is all black. Long-coated puppies also turn

up in litters and, although they are not suitable for showing or breeding, they make excellent pets and working dogs. Eight-week-old puppies, incidentally, do not have upright ears; the correct ear carriage develops later.

The medium-length coat has a dense harsh, outer layer which should lie flat against the body over a softer undercoat. This double coat acts as an efficient insulator against extremes of both heat and cold, enabling the breed to work in almost any climatic conditions. Grooming can be done on a table or with the dog standing on the floor, and the necessary equipment is a stiff bristle brush, a wide-toothed metal comb and a grooming glove. Brush with the lie of the coat in strong steady strokes. When the dog is moulting, you will need to use the comb to remove the loose undercoat. The grooming glove is used to give a final polish.

The temperament of an adult German Shepherd generally makes it somewhat aloof with strangers, but it should not be nervous or aggressive. Since temperament is of paramount importance in the companion animal, you should try to buy from a breeder who also considers this aspect important. You should also try to see one or both of the parents and observe if they are prepared to be friendly after the proper introductions have been made between you and the dog.

Hip Dysplasia, an inherited abnormality, fairly frequently occurs in German Shepherds. In the worst

cases the adult dog becomes lame and is in constant pain because of the malformation of the hip joints. The condition cannot often be diagnosed in a young puppy, and as the exact mode of inheritance is unknown, it is a condition that is unlikely to be eradicated from any breed in the forseeable future. However, serious breeders will take into account the hip conditions of their breeding stock when planning a mating, thus lessening the chance of producing afflicted offspring.

German Shepherds are active in both body and mind. Therefore, as well as adequate daily exercise, some form of training is really necessary for the dog's mental health. The breed is very well catered for with breed clubs and training societies who will welcome novice owners.

The Labrador Retriever

The Labrador originally came from the coasts of Newfoundland and is first mentioned in the early 1800s as being a type of dog kept by the deep sea fishermen of those rocky coasts. The dogs lived on the quays or tucked themselves aboard the fishing boats. They were expected to rescue anything which fell into the water, to take lines from boat to shore, and also to take the rope ends of the nets through the water to the men on shore, who could then haul the catch in without the boat having to make a dangerous landfall. The Labrador today is still an excellent swimmer, with a fondness for water and mud!

This strong, willing dog was at one time expected to earn its keep without being too fussy about its food or accommodation and was often called the St John's dog or the St John's Newfoundland. When the cod boats sailed to sell their catch in England, the dogs often went with them. As the cod boats used Poole Harbour, the breed became known in the Dorset area, and as sportsmen appreciated them for their retrieving abilities the fishermen often sold their dogs as well as the cod. A letter in the 1870s from the Earl of Malmsbury tells of his purchasing such a dog and says 'We always call mine Labradors', a name which stuck and distinguishes them from the giant Newfoundland breed. From about 1875 the breed gradually grew in numbers and popularity in Britain, whilst becoming virtually extinct in its homeland. The breed is now known worldwide, most countries having obtained their original stock from Britain.

Labradors are cheerful, obliging dogs with plenty of energy, especially when they are young. They are still widely used for retrieving game, both from the land and water, and are also

Below: *The Labrador Retriever's fondness of mud and water is a point to consider when choosing one for a pet.*

Right: *Black Labradors have always been the most popular in the shooting field but yellow Labradors seem to be the general public's favourites.*

used as police dogs, particularly in the field of drug detection. They are also one of the mainstays for the Guide Dogs for the Blind Association, who use more Labradors and Golden Retrievers than any other breeds. They are among the most popular of family dogs, and particularly suitable for energetic, outdoor-loving households with older children. Sufficient exercise is essential and, having been bred always to fetch and carry, the breed still has a very strong desire to use their mouths. It is for this reason that bored, unhappy Labradors when shut up for long periods on their own, can sometimes be extremely destructive.

The Labrador's coat is very short and dense, and feels hard to the touch. Its slight oiliness makes it waterproof. The original Labradors were black; yellows did not appear until the beginning of this century, although they are now the favourite colour with the public. Chocolate-coloured Labradors are rare, but this is also an acceptable colour.

Grooming is simple and you need little more than a soft bristle brush. Use a bit of pressure when brushing, as this stimulates the skin and most dogs love it. A final polish with a soft duster gives a bright sheen to the coat. Combing should only be necessary when the dog is moulting.

An effective method of grooming dogs with short coats is simply to use your hands. Rake your spread fingers through the coat, working from the tail towards the neck. This will loosen dead hair and scurf and the pressure of your finger tips will stimulate the blood circulation. Finally, smooth the coat flat with the palms of your hands to give the coat gloss. The most useful piece of equipment for drying wet and muddy dogs is a large chamois leather. Wring this out tightly in hot water and rub it over the coat, squeezing out the excess water at intervals. This will clean and dry a dog to the 'just damp' stage more effectively than any other course of action.

The Labrador requires plenty of good food during its growth period. Sadly, overweight pet Labradors are all too common a sight, their owners perhaps having confused excess flesh with the sturdy build of the breed. If you are unsure whether your dog is too fat, one simple way to check is to lay your hand flat on the ribcage. If your fingers have to dig through a layer of flab to feel the bones, the dog is overweight, a condition as bad for dogs as it is for humans.

Some pet Labradors are prone to skin troubles. These are very rarely seen on the working dog, which suggests that boredom and lack of exercise might be contributory factors. The Guide Dog Association reports that skin complaints amongst the Labradors they have trained are negligible. These dogs are engaged in doing worthwhile jobs and, moreover, their blind owners have been instructed to spend half an hour a day on grooming them.

The Cocker Spaniel

Someone once said that what a Cocker Spaniel does not communicate to you with its eyes it does with its tail. This goes some way to describing the attraction of this merry, busy and charmingly friendly dog. The Cocker Spaniel was the most popular breed in Britain during the 1940s and 1950s. Twenty-seven thousand Cocker puppies were registered with the Kennel Club in 1947, a breed statistic which has yet to be equalled. Furthermore, for seventeen years, from 1936 to 1952, they were at the top of the American Kennel Club registrations, longer than any other breed. Since then the Cocker has declined numerically from these heights, but it is still a well-loved favourite with many people.

The name 'Spaniel' has been in use for several centuries, but fifteenth- and sixteenth-century illustrations show dogs that look more like small setters than the modern spaniels. The dogs were reputed to come from Spain, as the name suggests, and the early writers describe the dogs as being used to hunt for game birds and water fowl, 'setting' and 'crouching' when they scented a covey, and finally 'springing'

Left: *The American Cocker Spaniel differs from the English variety in its high domed forehead and luxurious coat.*

Below: *Cocker Spaniels have been great favourites for many years. The golden colour of these puppies is just one of the many colours found in this breed.*

the birds into the air for waiting falcons or into a net spread by the huntsman. Although spaniels then were a working 'type' rather than a breed, the merrily wagging tails, busy manner and tendency to bark that are now characteristics of the breed were all much in evidence.

Spaniels as sporting dogs continued merely to be divided into rough categories of water and land spaniels until quite late in the nineteenth century. In 1870, the Kennel Club categorized everything together under the title Field Spaniel and divided them by weight into over and under 11 kg (25 lbs). By 1893 the smaller variety had become officially called Cocker Spaniels, a name derived from the fact that they were considered particularly suitable for flushing woodcock.

The Cocker Spaniel should be built so that it is capable of doing a day's work, which involves pushing through heavy cover to find game. In other words it tends to be a compact, strong dog for its size and weight and, although few are now used for work, most pets will still hunt with tireless persistence and great enjoyment, given the opportunity. The coat is flat and silky and may be a wide variety of colours, both whole and broken with flecks or patches of white.

A medium stiff brush should be used fairly vigorously on the coat. It is particularly important to get out the dead hair, otherwise the coat looks bunchy and dry instead of flat and silkily gleaming. The feet should be neatened by trimming round them with blunt-ended scissors, and the hair should also be snipped from between the toes. This helps to keep the foot compact and prevents the dog bringing too much mud indoors with it. Thinning scissors should be used on the feathering down the back of the legs and on the tops of the ears, to prevent it becoming too profuse. Some Cocker Spaniels have a tuft of rather woolly hair on the dome of their heads and this should be gently stripped away by pulling out the hairs. This is a very sensitive part of the dog however, so be very careful.

Cockers can suffer from ear troubles and the procedure detailed for Poodles should be followed. It is worth buying a deep, narrow feeding bowl so that the dog's ears do not get covered with food at each meal. Alternatively, the ears can be tucked into an old nylon stocking to keep them out of the way when the dog is fed. Cockers love comfort and food, and those beseeching eyes and gentle velvet mouth have tempted many an unwary owner into giving too many titbits, so make sure you watch your dog's waistline carefully.

Sadly there are some snappy and irritable little Cockers about, a travesty of the true breed temperament, so always try to buy a puppy from a sweet-tempered line.

The Cocker Spaniel type was very varied in America for a long time, a situation which was resolved in 1946 by the American Kennel Club recognizing the American Cocker Spaniel as a separate and distinct breed and it is the latter which is the American favourite. These dogs are rather smaller than their English counterpart. The muzzle is shorter and the skull domed, which gives them a rather more pert expression. The most noticeable difference, however, is the wealth of coat carried by the American Cocker which may fairly be said to be dripping glamour, in some cases with hair to the floor.

The Irish Setter
This big, handsome, boisterous dog is often called the Red Setter because of its gleaming, bright chestnut coat. The breed comes from Ireland and, in common with most Irish breeds, very little is known about its origin and possible ancestry.

Setting is an old term meaning the same as pointing – that is indicating where game is hidden by pausing and staring in that direction. Setting dogs have been used at least since mediaeval times to find game birds but the heyday of the Setters in the shooting fields came in the Victorian era. The landed gentry had big estates devoted to pheasant, grouse and partridge, and these provided the space which is really needed to work Setters effectively. The dog was expected to range in front of the guns, galloping across a wide strip of ground, which it gradually quartered so that every area was searched for sitting birds. When the dog caught the air scent of the game birds on the ground it froze into the classic position of a dog pointing

Right: *The handsome, boisterous Irish Setter is popularly nicknamed the Red Setter, because of its rich golden coat.*

game, the whole body rigid with expectation and one forepaw raised in the air. As the sportsman approached, the dog was urged to creep on until the birds broke cover and afforded a shot for the waiting game.

As the big shooting estates were sold or broken up there were fewer and fewer opportunities for Pointers and Setters to work. The Irish Setter had always been rather a controversial performer in the field, owing to a certain headstrong quality which is still apparent today. This means that, though known to be capable of giving brilliant performances, they were also considered rather unreliable, especially as they did not respond very well to the somewhat brutal methods of training used by Victorian gamekeepers. Although its use declined, the Irish Setter never really

went out of favour as a breed, its sweetness of expression and brilliant coat colouring consistently attracting new owners. Today it is an extremely popular pet and the best known of all members of the Setter family.

The dog is built on galloping lines and needs a good deal of exercise if only to work off some of that madcap exuberance. It responds very well to firm but kindly training, and really needs this to prevent its friendly boisterousness becoming a nuisance.

The moderately long coat is flat, gleaming and silky. The dog is now so identified with the red colouring that it is difficult to credit that red and white used to be equally common. The red and white colouring became so unfashionable at the beginning of this century that it is now never seen.

Coat care of the Setter is relatively

Above: *Pekingese are amongst the aristocrats of the dog world. Always dogs of great character, they usually have their owners well in hand rather than the other way about!*

Right: *A Chinese Empress described the colours of the Pekingese as follows: 'Let it be that of a lion – a golden sable, to be carried in the sleeve of a yellow robe, or the colour of a red bear, or striped like a dragon, so that there may be dogs appropriate to every costume in the Imperial wardrobe'. The Pekingese is sometimes known as the Lion or Dragon dog.*

simple. Brush it with a bristle brush, and use a metal comb on the feathering on the legs, the longer hair on the underside and the flag on the tail. Massage with a hound glove and polishing with a cloth or the bare hand will bring up the shine which makes this dog so spectacular.

56

The Pekingese

The romantic origins of this breed probably contributed to its early rise to popularity, although it is almost certainly its wealth of personality that has kept it in the forefront for so long. We know that the Chinese, who were very skilled animal breeders, have produced toy dogs for at least fifteen hundred years. Ownership of Pekingese was the prerogative of the Imperial family. Scroll paintings of the eighteenth century show graceful little dogs with elaborate belled collars very like today's breed of Pekingese, though with rather less coat. Much elaborate ritual concerned the care and breeding of such animals, particularly as the colours and coat markings were considered to have symbolic significance. The lion plays a great part in Buddhist legend, and many of the small dogs of both China and Tibet were meant to represent this mythical beast. We also know that very small dogs, known as sleeve dogs, were bred, which could nestle in the wide sleeves of their owners' gowns. The coat colours of these dogs were varied to suit their owners' extensive and luxurious wardrobes!

In 1860 a British military expedition sacked Peking. The Imperial Court had fled, taking their much-valued dogs with them, but five were accidentally left behind. These were taken to London, where the smallest of the four bitches was presented to Queen Victoria. The others were kept and bred by the Duchess of Richmond and it is from this nucleus, plus a very few later imports, that all the Pekingese in the Western Hemisphere are descended.

Any breed which gains royal patronage tends to become fashionable and the Pekingese was no exception. However, owners of the small animals found that they had a dog both stout-hearted and stubborn, a great individualist, immensely dignified when the occasion seemed to call for it but also fun-loving and playful. The Pekingese is a very strong-boned, heavy dog for its size and is one of the few breeds where the bitches are customarily slightly bigger than the dogs. The short, bowed forelegs (bred into the breed to prevent it straying far from the Imperial precincts) obviously preclude the dog from being the companion of an energetic hiker, but Pekingese are both active and surprisingly sporting characters given the chance. The coat can be almost any colour or combination of colours, and is long, straight and profuse, with rather a coarse-textured top coat and a thick undercoat. There should be a good mane of hair forming a cape round the neck and plenty of feathering on the ears, legs and tail.

The secret of keeping the Pekingese's coat in good order is brushing, brushing and yet more brushing. If taught to do so as puppies, most Pekingese accept this with equanimity, lying on their owners laps to be brushed in any position in which they are placed. The brush should be bristle, the best and most expensive of ladies' hair-brushes being ideal. Combing should be done sparingly, as it will in time reduce the density of the coat by taking too much out (although some pet owners might not consider this a disadvantage). Pekingese should be bathed only very rarely, but swabbing of the under-parts is sometimes necessary. Use tepid water and cotton wool to do this, then dry the hair very thoroughly and dust it with a little baby powder.

Some Pekingese grow a great deal of hair on their feet, so much so that it should be trimmed away for their own comfort. Great care must be taken when grooming round the eyes as, with all breeds where these are large and prominent, they are susceptible to injury. Even a slight knock or scratch on the eye can lead to ulceration. The simplest eyewash to float foreign bodies out of the eye is a saline solution made by dissolving one teaspoon of cooking salt (i.e. iodine free salt) in 600 ml (1 pint) of boiling water. Allow the solution to cool to body temperature and apply it by soaking a pad of cottonwool in the liquid and squeezing this so that the solution trickles across the eyeball.

The creases and wrinkles in the facial skin of a Pekingese also need care as they must be kept clean and dry. As air cannot reach the skin here, sores can develop. Prevention of these consists of keeping the area clean and making sure that the wrinkles are dry by using a very light sprinkling of unperfumed talcum or baby powder.

With all toy dogs the teeth are usually very crowded in the mouth, and tend therefore to become dirty and finally decayed. This trouble is often aggravated by the tendency of the owners of small dogs to feed them either pappy or finely minced food. As anyone who has ever been bitten by a small dog will be able to testify, not only are the teeth quite sharp, the jaw power is also quite considerable! Large uncooked bones, such as marrow bones, are as acceptable to small dogs as to large ones, and provide much healthy exercise for teeth and gums. If your small dog will not eat dog biscuits (and some are a little fussy in this respect) then dried rusks or wholemeal bread may be an acceptable substitute for this part of the diet. Above all, do not feed sticky mixtures which will

adhere to the teeth and gums.

Many of the flat-faced breeds, of which the Pekingese is one, suffer in the heat. Given the chance they will find their own cool spot in hot weather, and I have even seen a Peke dig a shallow hole on a beach in order to lie more comfortably in cool, damp sand. An electric fan is a help, and a rubber hot water bottle filled with crushed ice and wrapped in towels, placed in the dog's basket, can be a help in giving it somewhere cool to lie. Alternatively, the hot water bottle can be partly filled with water and placed in the freezer compartment of a fridge to solidify before being used as above.

The Dachshund

The Dachshund is possibly the most versatile of companion dogs. Although it can be a variety of sizes and colours, with different types of coats, the shape of the long, low body on short, heavily boned legs is unmistakable. Its many caricatures and nicknames are perhaps a measure of the amused esteem in which the breed is held.

Long, low-legged hounds have been known on the continent of Europe since at least the Middle Ages, but the Dachshund proper is a German breed, originally a forester's dog used for hunting. The name means 'badger hound'. These dogs, admirably designed for wriggling through crevices and down burrows, were expected to enter the badger's set, keep the beast at bay and, by keeping up a continuous noise, indicate to

those waiting above where both it and its quarry were under the ground, so that the badger could be dug out and killed. Dachshunds were also expected to bolt rabbits, tackle foxes or anything else underground, as well as tracking anything from roe deer downwards or ranging and flushing game from areas of undergrowth. The Germans bred a range of sizes from the little rabbit hounds upwards, but in Britain two sizes only are recognized: miniatures, which weigh about 4.5 kg (10 lb) and standards, which weigh about 9 kg (20 lbs).

Dachshunds, then, are hunting hounds, vociferous because they were required to bay when following a scent or finding a quarry, and with good noses. Like all the scent hounds they can be a little stubborn, for a dog puzzling out a cold line needs to be deaf to most distractions. The broad, velvety paws are good at digging, which was necessary for its underground pursuits. These outdoor qualities are combined with a playful and affectionate nature and a sybaritic love of comfort and good food. If it is given the opportunity, the warmest and most comfortable place in the house will be where this little dog sleeps, just as it will accurately assess

Right: *Given the chance, Dachshunds are very sporting little dogs. These two are the miniature smooth-haired variety, once used to hunt rabbits.*

Below: *The standard long-haired Dachshund is extremely popular.*

the person likely to have the weakest will at a meal table and sit confidingly by his or her chair!

There are three coat varieties in the Dachshund – smooth, long and wire – and almost any colour except white is permissible. The two commonest colours are red and black and tan. The smooth-coated dog requires little grooming other than massage with a hound glove and a final polish. The long-coated variety first appeared in Britain in the 1920s, and quickly attracted attention because of its glamour. The coat is soft and slightly waved and described as of 'shining colour'. The feathering is abundant on the ears, legs, under parts and the tail. A bristle brush of medium soft texture should be used in grooming, and the feathering combed regularly to prevent any tangling. Some of this variety grow too much hair on their feet for their own comfort and it should be trimmed away.

The wire-haired Dachshund needs rather more attention to its coat than the other two varieties, which may well be the reason why it has not achieved their popularity. The coat should be short and harsh, with an undercoat. The ears are smooth and the dog should have a beard and bushy eyebrows. Ordinary care consists of brushing regularly and vigorously with the bristle brush. However, two or three times a year the coat will require stripping out; this means taking off the old topcoat to expose the undercoat, thus allowing the new harsh coat to grow through. The technique is best learnt by watching someone experienced at work. Alternatively the dog can be taken to a beauty parlour when necessary.

Dachshunds tend to be greedy, the sad result of which is that there are many obese dogs. There is no more pitiful sight than seeing a dog which should be a trim and muscular animal waddling dispiritedly along. Very overweight animals should be taken to a veterinary surgeon who, after checking the animal's general health, can prescribe an obesity diet. The merely plump should have the carbohydrate cut from their diet and a multivitamin supplement added. Remember that a dog being slimmed down will be hungrier, and therefore more liable to steal or to beg persistently for the forbidden titbits.

Sadly too, the shape of Dachshunds predisposes them to slipped discs. This condition can usually be treated successfully, but may need prolonged and sympathetic nursing, since the animal can be paralysed for a number of weeks. The likelihood of this condition occurring can be aggravated by the dog being overweight.

The Rough Collie
It seems likely that all the Collie breeds originated in Scotland. The Rough Collie developed from the shepherding dogs that are valued wherever sheep play an important part in the economy. These working Collies of the late eighteenth and early nineteenth century were probably a mixed lot, because working ability rather than looks was the criterion of their worth. All, however, were expected to stand up to the worst of weather, cover great distances over punishing country and exist on a very poor diet.

The emergence of the Rough Collie from this background was partly due to the royal patronage of Queen Victoria. On one of her many visits to the Highlands of Scotland she

acquired one of these heavily coated sheepdogs, and grew so attached to it that thereafter some were always kept in her kennels. By the 1880s a boom in Rough Collies was under way, with high prices being paid on both sides of the Atlantic for good specimens. The farmers and shepherds referred to the new show Collies as 'improved Collies' when compared with the unimproved working types. The improved Collies were larger and carried a more profuse coat, with a much accentuated mane and frill on the chest and round the neck. The head became more refined and the distinctive ear carriage was standardized. Temperament changed, too. Many of the farmer's dogs were sharp and suspicious in nature while the Rough Collie, though still sometimes aloof with strangers, is much loved for its sweet character.

Of course, all changes are not necessarily for the better and the Rough Collie today makes no pretence of being a working sheepdog. However, the glamour of the magnificent coat, combined with a biddable nature, have kept this elegant and dignified breed as public favourites.

The three recognized colours are sable and white, tricolour and blue merle. Sable can be any shade from light gold to rich mahogany, set off by a white chest and frill and often a full white collar. Blue Merle have always been in a minority as this is a difficult shade to breed. The colour should be clear, silvery blue, splashed and marbled with black and set off by rich tan markings. The coat should always be dense and harsh and is brushed outwards to help the hair stand away from the body. A medium bristle brush should be used, the coat being parted and brushed in layers. Combing with a coarse comb should be done in moderation after brushing. Occasionally the feet may need trimming to neaten the outline.

The Shetland Sheepdog
The Shetland Sheepdog is as popular as his bigger cousin the Collie. This breed in its present form is a product of

Left: *The Shetland Sheepdog is the smaller version of the Rough Collie.*

Above: *A Golden Retriever bitch lies quietly with her young puppy. This dog has proved to be one of the most adaptable of all gundog breeds.*

the twentieth century, although the diminutive working dogs of the Shetland Isles obviously have a much longer history. Early tourists brought the small working dogs of the Islands back to the mainland. They were not so heavily coated as today's Sheltie and varied a great deal in type. Controversy immediately broke out between those who wished to keep the working type and those who wished to glamorize them. The latter faction won, so that today's Sheltie resembles a Rough Collie in miniature. It is a dainty little dog, gentle, loyal and affectionate. Some are a little retiring in nature, so it is wise to pick a bold puppy. The colours and the coat care are the same as for its larger relative.

The Golden Retriever
This active and well balanced dog, whose practical use as a working gundog has perforce declined in this century, has found a new role as a guide dog for the blind and also as a very widely kept and highly valued companion dog. The breed has a kindly expression which is not belied by its nature, and its intelligence and willingness to please make it easy to train. Like all the powerfully built retrieving breeds, the Golden Retriever needs a reasonable amount of daily exercise to keep it happy.

The Golden Retriever was developed as a working gundog by the Majoribanks family in the second half of the nineteenth century. The main breeding stock were Flat-coated Retrievers, which were then the most popular variety. As also happened in Labradors, black flat-coated parents occasionally had a yellow puppy, and one of these, mated to a Tweed Spaniel, provided the foundation stock for the new breed. (The Tweed Spaniel is one of many extinct breeds, and as no known illustration exists we can only speculate as to its looks.)

The coat of a Golden Retriever should be flat to the body, with a slight waviness. The undercoat is water-resistant. The deep, burnished gold colour is sadly becoming rarer as the lighter shades of cream become increasingly popular. Grooming should be done with a bristle brush used fairly vigorously in order to get down to the skin. The feathering down the back of the legs and under the tail should be combed with a metal comb.

Working dogs

It is probably only within the last century that more dogs have been kept for the pleasure they give and their general companionship than have been kept as working animals. Industrialization and technology have removed the need to use dogs in many spheres where they have been working for centuries. The development of road and rail transport has drastically reduced the numbers of droving dogs who, before the age of mechanized transport, moved sheep and cattle along the highways and byways to market and slaughter. The roasting

Left: *The Border Collie is one of the most widely used of working sheepdogs. Many do not make suitable pets unless given an outlet for their brains and energy.*

Below: *Many breeds of shaggy sheepdogs, such as this Italian Bergamese sheepdog, come from Europe. Others are the Briard and Bearded Collie.*

spit is now turned by electricity rather than by a small dog running inside a wheel-shaped treadmill. The decline in the numbers of large predators in many parts of the world means that there is less need for large guard dogs prepared to defend their master's livestock and property against wolves and other marauders.

Although it would be possible to go on citing such instances until one reached the conclusion that the day of the working dog is over, this would be somewhat premature. Man is continually finding new uses for his oldest friend, and it seems unlikely that the working dog will be replaced entirely by the machine in the foreseeable future.

The daily life of the four different working dogs described in this chapter may differ widely, but some basic similarities exist, necessary factors in a successful working partnership

Prince Rupert to the rescue

I had a dog called Prince Rupert, a big, strong, curly, brown retriever, brother to King Koffee, who was the champion curly retriever in this country and the father of all the best for years. I kept Prince Rupert on the marsh because he was essentially a very strong dog and a marsh dog. He could stand any amount of work, like I was able to myself... It had been cold for several days, and was still freezing, but it was too rough for the ice to settle down on that water. In the dark I couldn't tell whether it was water or ice; I only knew that the keepers reported a good many fowl about in the morning, so I went down to see what I could get. They came over now and then, and I got seven or eight down. Some fell on to the water and some on the land. It gradually got light, and then I saw that the water was covered with ice, but it could not be thick, because on the previous day there had been none, and it was now unduly thickened through the water's previous readiness to freeze. Prince Rupert was a little out of condition, but he knew my signals, and when the time came to retrieve these birds there was a teal lying on the ice about fifty yards out. I pointed it out to Prince, and he went for it. He dashed through the sedges, and made his way to the bird. The ice was not thin enough for him to swim through; he had to fight his way through it with his forelegs.

When within about a yard of it he was exhausted, but, craning his neck over the ice, he kept making futile attempts to get the bird. He would not turn back, but presently lay perfectly still on the top of the water. My two keepers were coming up to join me, and they arrived at that moment. Of course, it meant drowning. I asked the men if they could suggest anything, and there was no rope, no boat, no anything. The water was deep. I was frantic. The poor dog was out there with not much of a kick left in him, yet even then he tried to crane his neck to get the bird.

'I'm d----d if I'm going to see the dog drown,' I suddenly exclaimed. I chucked off my coat and waistcoat, and dashed into the sedges until I got to the edge of the ice. The first part of the ice broke by my trying to get on to it, but I went a little wide and to my great astonishment I succeeded in getting on an ice raft. It was floating, but it proved sufficient to bear me. I kept away from the rill the dog had made in going out, and I bent down and gradually worked the floating ice by swaying my body until I got opposite to Prince. I then got hold of his topknot and worked back with him in just the same way.

When we got within a yard or two of the bank the whole contraption gave way, but of course I could struggle out. The dog was apparently dead. Coated with ice, he was an ice-dog – ice all over him in a great, big mass. We had to kick it off him. We carried him down to the decoy house, laid him in front of the fire, gave him brandy, kept rubbing him, of course, – and he lived for years after.

Extract from Dr Salter, His Diary and Reminiscences from the Year 1849 to 1932
This incident took place in the 1880s.

the Search and Rescue Dog Association. Increased leisure time and improved transportation means that more and more people are enjoying the pleasures of hill-walking and mountain-climbing. Even the experienced can get into trouble in such country, however, and the number of people lost or injured tends to rise each year. The idea of using dogs to find people buried in avalanches originated in Switzerland and has been practised there for a number of years, mainly using German Shepherd dogs.

Speed is the essential factor in rescuing people buried in snow. If found within 30 minutes the victim has a 90 per cent chance of survival, but after five hours it has dropped to 30 per cent. The speed with which a trained dog can locate a buried victim in favourable circumstances has been demonstrated by a volunteer being buried in a 20 metre (25 yard) square of snow. It took a line of men equipped with long probes (the traditional method of finding avalanche victims) 28 minutes to detect him and it took a man with a mine detector nine minutes to locate someone buried in a similar area. The dog, however, took a mere 30 seconds to scent the victim and indicate his position by digging down to him through the snow.

The Search and Rescue Dog Association was formed in 1965 and is manned entirely by volunteers. Both the men and their dogs are rigorously screened before being accepted for training. The Association runs its own tests to grade the dogs, which have to be fit and agile enough to cover the roughest of country, have the build and coat to withstand the worst the weather can offer, be dependable with livestock and totally non-aggressive. Breeds used successfully for this work include German Shepherds, various Collies and Retrievers and Elkhounds. All are taught to search an area of ground methodically by working in wide arcs across wind, until they pick up a scent which they then follow up-wind to the victim.

One of the difficulties in training a dog for this work is that a search may go on for hour after hour without anybody being found. Novice and inexperienced dogs get discouraged by this and tend to give up unless they have the stimulus of a success to keep up their interest. Indicating when they

between man and dog. The dog has to be physically suited to the work expected of it, which means having both energy and stamina as well as being of a suitable size. It has to be temperamentally sound so that it is capable of learning and will be reliable under pressure. It must also have the ability to concentrate on the job in hand under all circumstances.

Training in nearly all working dogs begins with the simple obedience exercises which every pet dog should be taught. These simple foundations provide the groundwork for everything which is to follow, but

intensive and specialized training does not start until the dog is adult and mature enough to concentrate. Every lesson is broken down into small stages, each of which has to be thoroughly mastered before anything else is taught. In many ways consistency of the dog's performance will reflect the consistency and the thoroughness of its training, a training that has to be carried out in such a way that the dog remains enthusiastic and gets its reward from the satisfaction of pleasing its trainer.

One of the newest organizations in Britain that depends on trained dogs is have found something can also be a problem. Most dogs are taught to stay close to the victim and to bark, but this may not always be heard when the weather is particularly wild. Some dogs, while excellent at searching, are extremely reluctant to give tongue when they have found somebody. Such animals are generally taught to return to their handler, who is able to judge from the dog's behaviour whether it has been successful or not in its search. In Germany a different method is used. A short strap, which in no way impedes the dog's progress, hangs from a swivel on its collar. The dog is taught to take the strap in its mouth when it makes a find and return to its handler, who can then be sure that the dog has been successful and will lead him in the direction of the lost person.

Fully trained Search and Rescue dogs may be called upon at any time, and it is an unwritten rule of the Association that the volunteers who man it will answer calls for assistance whenever they arise. The dogs themselves are basically companion animals, whose owners are responsible for keeping them fully fit and fully trained. To ensure that the standard is maintained, testing is done at intervals. The calls made on the Search and Rescue Dog Association increase annually, but expansion depends on attracting the right volunteers with suitable dogs and also on forthcoming funds, for this Association is financed entirely by public donations.

The police dog is a more familiar working animal, although surprisingly enough the British police took a long time, compared with some of the continental police forces, to realize the potential of trained dogs. The most popular breed for police work is the German Shepherd and the best age for intensive training is considered to be between twelve and eighteen months. The police run their own breeding

Above right and right: Highly trained guard dogs are for specialists only since they can be a potential danger in inexperienced hands. German Shepherds are the mainstay of the world's police forces. They are suitable for work in any climate and have the necessary strength and agility for active service. The dog should not be aggressive or shy but have a natural suspicion of strangers. This watchfulness is among their most valuable assets and makes them much sought after as working dogs.

programme, since a higher proportion of trainable dogs will come from parents who have been selected for their working abilities. Suitable animals donated by the public are also accepted for training, however. The dogs live with their handlers and both train together for a three-month period. Both also attend refresher courses throughout their working partnership, since a dog learns by repetition and will forget acquired skills if it is called upon to use them only rarely.

Police dogs are expected to perform a variety of duties, for too much specialization would be uneconomic. They are particularly valuable in dealing with rowdy behaviour, and in searching premises for hidden intruders. They are also used for tracking after a crime has been committed, for the recovery of missing articles and in the search for missing people. In other words, a lot of police work involves utilizing the dog's remarkable powers of scent, the best example of this being the specially trained drug-detection dogs. It has been calculated that a well trained dog can replace twenty men when searching an area and still do the job

more quickly and efficiently.

'Manwork' – that is the stopping and holding of a fleeing criminal – has to be taught with great care, since it poses a number of difficulties. A highly trained dog of dependable temperament is extremely reluctant to bite, and this inhibition has to be broken down. Once this has been done, particular attention has to be paid to ensuring that the dog works on the handler's command only, since the sight of someone running or behaving in a furtive manner must not trigger the dog into pursuit. Finally, the dog must leave hold instantly on command, something which an animal excited by a struggle will be loath to do. A dog of the right temperament will be fearless and aggressive when required, but perfectly relaxed and dependable in normal circumstances. This aspect of the dog's character is not always appreciated by the general public.

A dog on the beat will work an eight-hour day. It is most usual, however, for dog patrols to be equipped with vans so that the animals can be sent quickly to places where their particular talents may be required. A police dog will continue working until slowed down by old age, and the average working

life is about eight years.

Labradors and Golden Retrievers provide most of the guide dogs for the blind and, again, the Association finds it most satisfactory to breed their own stock from carefully selected parents. Any suitable dog will be accepted for training, provided it passes the very rigorous screening. It must be at least 58 cm (19 ins) at the shoulder, be between ten months and two and a half years old, be friendly and fully acquainted with town conditions and family life. Bitches are preferred for training and make up about three-quarters of the work force. All the bitches are spayed and all the males castrated, which gives the lie to the quite widely held belief that neutered animals invariably become lethargic, dull-witted and obese.

The guide dog starts its training with the same simple obedience exercises that precede all advanced work; that is, to come, to sit, to lie down and to stay on command. It is also taught to walk in the correct position, which is on the left-hand side and slightly ahead of the person it is leading. The dog is then introduced to the harness and learns to differentiate between the responsibilities of work when the harness is on and the relaxation permitted when it is off. As well as learning directional commands, the dog learns to avoid obstacles on its own initiative and also to allow for the height and the width of the person being led in all circumstances. Learning to cross busy roads safely is possibly one of the most demanding exercises that a guide dog performs, since it has to ignore commands that would take its blind owner into danger. In effect, the animal is taught that a moving vehicle within a certain distance is a signal to stop or to disregard the command 'Forward' given by its owner, while a stationary vehicle within the same distance is not.

Above left: *A trained guide dog gives a blind man the freedom of movement that the rest of us take for granted. This is one of the most responsible and exacting jobs that a dog can do and each animal is carefully tested for its suitability before being trained.*

Right: *The elegant Rough Collie is rarely used as a working sheepdog, nowadays, but makes a superb domestic pet. It is easy to train and soon becomes an obedient companion.*

Not all blind applicants are considered suitable for a guide dog. The owner must be physically active and also motivated by a strong desire for independence, for it is this that provides the stimulus that will help him or her to learn to use the dog correctly, and ultimately to have complete confidence in the animal's actions. The personality of the blind person and that of the guide dog are assessed, so that as far as it is possible to predict the two will form a complementary partnership. They then do a month's training together, during which time they will board public transport, go shopping and generally be encouraged to live a normal, independent existence.

The working life of a guide dog is about nine years, and those people who have had a dog and need a replacement go to the top of the very long waiting list. The dogs themselves have a really remarkable record for reliability, and there are a number of instances on record where they have pushed or pulled their owners out of dangerous situations, apparently comprehending the limitations of human sightlessness instinctively.

The training of a working sheepdog is a rather different matter from the types of training that have already been outlined. The main reason for this is that working sheepdogs have a strong instinctive drive to round up livestock and their training consists more of controlling and harnessing this instinct than teaching them the process step by step. Indeed, no shepherd would bother to proceed with a dog that did not show this instinct to herd, although the age when it develops varies between individual animals. Border Collies, active and agile in both mind and body, are the premier sheepdogs. A Border Collie pup may start to show the desire to round up anything that moves as early as three months of age. In others, the instinct may not start to show until they are beginning to mature.

Before serious training can start, the dog must be old enough to be physically able to deal with the work it is expected to learn. It must also come when called, and drop flat and stay down on command. The first aim is to get the dog to run round a flock of sheep, which most will do quite instinctively. Patient training then refines the dog's technique so that it swings out in a wide arc that will not panic the sheep away from the shepherd or the direction he wants him to go. The dog is also taught to go to the left or right on command. A good sheepdog will keep the sheep going smoothly in the required direction, never causing them to panic and always ready to streak after those that break away from the flocks.

Different types of work are naturally expected from sheepdogs in different areas. Some will be expected to gather sheep from the hills and fell-sides and bring them down to the men waiting in the valleys. Others will be working the sheep at much closer quarters, penning and shedding them, or moving the flock from field to field as directed. Few dogs can be expected to be equally good at both kinds of work, but whatever his speciality, a good dog should be able to cover anything between 30–60 kilometres (20–40 miles) on a working day, without tiring, however rough the country and hard the going may be under foot.

Exotic dogs

Man has always had an interest in the unusual and bizarre. Rarities of all sorts have commanded attention, although in some historical records it can be difficult to sift the evidence sufficiently to decide what is factual and what is hyperbolic. With regard to dogs, we do know for certain that very small or very large dogs, very aggressive or courageous ones, and those with specialized hunting abilities have always been considered valuable commodities. For centuries they were taken along the ancient trade routes of the world or sent as suitable presents from the courts of one sovereign ruler to another. Then, as now, novelty made news.

The dog is the domestic animal in which the widest variety of type exists. Dogs can vary in weight from 1 to 56 kg

Left: The glamorous Shih Tzu originally came from Tibet. The hair on the head should give a chrysanthemum-like effect to the face.

Below: The Japanese Chin is a dainty oriental toy dog.

(2 to 120 lbs), yet to the scientist they are all one species, probably descended from a common ancestor. It is difficult for the layman to understand how such wide differences of type can exist in a single species, especially since the genetic material passed on from parent to offspring is subject to very little change. Very occasionally, however, genes mutate – that is, a change occurs in the gene structure of a reproductive cell. Little is known about what causes it, although radiation is known to increase the incidence. Mutations are seldom beneficial in populations of wild animals, and the survival rate is low. However domestic dogs are a protected population, in which mutations affecting size, body shape, coat, colouring and other physical features can survive and become established as normal.

If the dog was domesticated some 10,000 years ago, then a statistical theory advanced by a geneticist decrees that only ten mutations in that period of time would give 1,024

different forms of shape and coat colour, provided each mutation affected both shape and colour. The wolf, believed to be the ancestor of the dog, also shows quite a wide variation of size and colour in the wild. It is easy to understand why there are so many breeds of dog differing so widely in size, shape and colouring.

Amongst the rarities of the dog world, it is perhaps the hairless breeds that have pride of place. It is not known what causes this condition, but hairless dogs have been quite widely distributed in the past in tropical and semi-tropical countries including Africa, Argentina, the West Indies and Mexico. A little over a century ago, hairless dogs were mentioned as being comparatively common along the Mexican–United States border and today the Mexican Kennel Club recognizes one hairless breed with the totally unpronounceable name of Kloloitzcuintli. The skin of this animal is a uniform dark bronze or elephant grey and, without the insulating covering of hair, feels hot to the touch. This fact possibly accounts for the belief in the past that these dogs had miraculous healing powers, as demonstrated in Jamaica, where hairless dogs were known as 'fever dogs' and were stretched across the body of the sufferer apparently to neutralize the fever.

The Chinese Crested Dog is the only hairless breed established in Britain, where it has a small but constant following. It is a toy breed, weighing up to 5 kg (12 lbs) and it actually has a crest of hair on the head and a plume of hair on the tail. The skin can be any colour, but is usually mottled with grey and pink, rather like the bark of a plane tree. Although it is an active and graceful little dog, its lack of coat means that not only must it be protected from the cold, but also from sunburn and any substances liable to set up skin allergies.

At the other extreme are those dogs whose length and density of coat are quite remarkable. This is particularly notable in two Hungarian breeds, the Komondor and the Puli, both of which are present in small numbers in Britain. The Komondor is a very large white dog used as a guard for the cattle and sheep that graze on the Hungarian plains. The exceptionally long and profuse coat hangs in cords and felted mats almost to the ground, thus providing almost complete protection against extremes of weather and external injury, but it is also an excellent hiding place for skin

parasites. These must be searched for and treated accordingly.

The Puli is a medium-sized dog with the agility and intelligence necessary to any breed whose primary work is controlling large flocks of sheep. The coat is usually black, and hangs in long cords that develop a rusty tinge as the animal becomes older. The hair totally obscures the animal's shape, and when the dog moves the hair swings like an old lady's voluminous skirts, gathering leaves and other debris. Puli owners claim, however, that looking after the coat is not a great chore. Puppies have short, fluffy hair and as this lengthens, it twists into cords which grow longer as the animal matures. Once the coat is corded, the dog cannot be brushed or combed, but it can be bathed. This is obviously a major operation and one that is unlikely to be tackled by the average owner as frequently as might reasonably be considered to be necessary and yet it is vital for hygiene and health reasons.

Neither Komondors or Pulis appear to suffer unduly in the heat, thereby providing a good illustration of the fact that hair not only insulates against extremes of cold but also protects against the effects of direct sunlight and hot weather.

Deep skin creases, such as those on the heads of Bloodhounds or Bulldogs, are even more of a feature in a breed like the Sharpeis. This dog appears to have a skin several sizes too large for its body, and it is covered by

accordian-like pleats and folds. The breed is reputed to come from China and a handful have reached the United States, although, it would seem, in too small a number to expect them to become established as a recognized or popular breed.

Amongst the toy breeds, which have been valued as amusing companions down the centuries, a number of attempts have been made to breed dogs resembling other animals. The Pekingese, the Shih Tzu and the Lhasa Apso were all endeavours to symbolize the lion of Buddha, although the lion was an animal unknown in the Chinese and Tibetan homelands of these breeds. Various small European breeds have also been referred to as lion dogs, usually because their coats were clipped in a fashion that left a mane and a tufted tail tip. The Lowchen is the modern example of this practice.

Other small dogs were valued because of their resemblance to monkeys and a number of them can be seen in paintings of the Renaissance period, often wearing belled or ornamental collars. Their modern equivalent is the Affenpinscher (the German name meaning 'monkey terrier'). This small black dog has a pair of brilliant dark eyes which sparkle with mischief and humour. These, together with its air of comic seriousness, its prominent bearded chin, moustache and beetling brows, combine to give a simian impression. It is quite a popular breed on the

Above and below left: The naked appearance of the Chinese Crested Dog is not to everybody's taste. However, they are quite robust and alert little dogs that have the advantage of being odourless. Despite the name no one knows quite how they originated, although hairless breeds like this one have been known and prized for many centuries. The skin can be any colour, either plain or spotted.

Right: The Puli is a nimble and agile dog with a sturdy muscular frame under that wealth of coat. Having been used as a herding dog on the Hungarian plains, the Puli is intelligent and responsive. Although renowned for being extremely independent, the Puli also makes a good 'town' pet. It is sometimes used by the police force, too, as a working dog.

continent; it is known in America and is just beginning to become established in Britain, although it will take sometime for the dog to become in any way well known.

Organized dog fighting has always been a widespread gambling sport and continues in many parts of the world today, satisfying man's perpetual interest in violence and cruelty. A number of specific types of dog were bred for fighting and also for baiting such unfortunate animals as bears, lions and bulls. All these breeds are distinguished by their undoubted courage, their aggression and an apparent insensitivity to pain. Oddly enough, many of them are particularly sweet-tempered towards the human race, and many current owners feel that the dog's loyalty is more than compensation for the responsibility of owning an animal that tends to look

Blue-tongued breed

My near neighbour, a young gentleman in the service of the East India Company, has brought home a dog and a bitch of the Chinese breed from Canton, such as are fattened in that country for the purpose of being eaten. They are about the size of a moderate spaniel; of a pale yellow colour, with coarse bristling hairs on their backs; sharp upright ears; and peaked heads, which give them a very fox-like appearance. Their hind legs are unusually straight, without any bend at the hock or ham, to such a degree as to give them an awkward gait when they trot. When they are in motion their tails are curved high over their backs like those of some hounds, and have a bare place each on the outside from the tip midway, that does not seem to be a matter of accident, but somewhat singular. Their eyes are jet-black, small and piercing; the insides of their lips and mouths of the same colour, and their tongues blue. The bitch has a dew-claw on each hind leg; the dog has none. When taken out into the field the bitch showed some disposition for hunting, and dwelt on the scent of a covey of partridges till she sprung them, giving her tongue all the time. The dogs in South America are dumb; but these bark much in a short thick manner like foxes, and have a surly, savage demeanor like their ancestors, which are not domesticated but bred up in sties, where they are fed for the table with rice-meal and other farinaceous food. These dogs, having been taken on board as soon as weaned, could not learn much from their dam; yet they did not relish flesh when they came to England.

Letter from Gilbert White to Daines Barrington, published December 1788.

for trouble when the opportunity presents itself.

One of the more spine-chilling of these breeds is the Chinese Fighting Dog, a very tough-skinned animal covered in harsh bristles. Its jaws are blunt and the big canine teeth, used for gripping and tearing, are curved like scimitars instead of being straight as they are in most breeds of dog. Despite this somewhat aggressive and off-putting appearance, they are reputed to be entirely amiable towards the human race.

There are of course many specialized hunting dogs extant in the world, but one of the rarest and the most unusual must be the Lundehund or Puffin Dog from Norway. This dog does not have a very distinguished appearance, being about 35 cm (14 ins) high and having a reddish or grey harsh top coat and a thick weatherproof undercoat. It was used to collect fledgling Puffins from the rocky burrows and inaccessible crevices where they nest; the down and feathers of these fledglings provided the islanders off the coast of Norway with a source of income. The unique feature of these dogs is that they have an extra toe on each foot, giving them a particularly broad paw. This helps them to gain footholds in the most difficult of terrains. The dog apparently locates the young birds by sound, undoubtedly aided by its very large, mobile ears, which it can fold and effectively close when pushing through narrow fissures. Unfortunately epidemics of distemper almost wiped the breed out, but determined efforts by Norwegian enthusiasts to preserve it are beginning to show some success and the dogs are generally becoming rather more widespread in that country, although they are still virtually unknown elsewhere in the world.

Few, if any, of the breeds described here are liable to become very popular. Some are unlikely to survive at all, as their breeding population is now so small that they are extremely vulnerable to disease or fertility problems. However, although their appeal may be limited, their distinctive peculiarities make an interesting catalogue of the oddities that can be perpetuated by selective breeding and also provide further evidence of the infinite variety that can be found amongst the great number of species of dogs living in the different countries throughout the world today.

The world of the dog

To gain some understanding of the dog, it is necessary to have some idea of the limitations of its senses and perception. To the dog the most important sense is that of smell. As sight is our most developed sense, it is difficult for us to appreciate how much of the dog's knowledge of the world about it is gained through its nose. For this reason, dogs adapt very well to the handicap of blindness and many owners can be quite unaware of it when their dog gradually loses its sight. A blind dog may continue to be able to retrieve a ball, apparently locating it by sound and smell. Man has always put the dog's superior sense of smell to his own use and dogs have been trained to locate a wide variety of objects for man's benefit, from edible fungi such as truffles, through to mines in a minefield or hidden drugs in a cargo. A dog concentrating on a track may be so absorbed in following its nose that it literally falls over the object of its search before its eyes register the find.

Since the sense of smell is closely allied with that of taste we must presume that this too is superior to ours. We know that a dog tracking something also produces extra saliva, thus enabling the minute scent-bearing particles to be savoured on the tongue as well as sniffed by the nose. The dog's hearing is more sensitive than ours and it can hear a wider range of sound. Of course, no dog understands every word you say, although you may teach it to associate a certain sound with a certain action. What the dog does hear are nuances of tone of which you may be unaware. A nervous person saying 'Good boy' to a dog may be conveying more of his fear than his good intentions to the animal. People with very flat monotonous voices often find training their dog quite difficult since the dog is unable to distinguish by their tone whether it is doing right or wrong. It is

Left: *The statuesque pose of the Pointer on scenting game is an instinctive response encouraged by careful training.*

Above: *The Dobermann is one of the most alert guard dogs. If well-trained, it also makes an excellent, loyal and obedient companion.*

quite common for dogs to be able to distinguish the sound of their owner's car from a medley of other traffic noises and this ability of the animal to hear the approach of something long before it is perceptible to a human makes them valuable as sentries, watch dogs and border patrol guards. Because their hearing is so sensitive a number of dogs are 'sound shy', that is sensitive and afraid of some noises, to which they will never be accustomed. In many cases training and familiarity with the frightening sound will produce indifference in the dog to the noise, but in some dogs this fear is an inherited trait that is too deeply rooted to be overcome.

From the structure of its eye, we must assume that the dog sees only in black and white. The dog cannot move its eyeballs as freely in the sockets as we can but compensates for this by having a longer, more mobile neck and moving its head more frequently. It is movement that attracts a dog's attention to an object some distance away, and it is remarkably difficult to point out a stationary object to a dog. Experience may finally teach it that your gesture means that it could be worthwhile to go and investigate with its nose. One other simple fact that is often overlooked when considering the dog's field of vision is the limitations imposed on its sight by its height from the ground.

Every dog is an individual who lives for the present and has no thought for the future. Like people, many of its actions are governed by instinct and past experience. It is by understanding these instinctive drives, and providing the experiences which either reinforce or inhibit them, that an animal can be trained to behave to suit its owner. A dog will tend not to repeat experiences which it finds unpleasant. You must of course also remember that a dog may find some experiences pleasant which we would not regard as agreeable. For example, some dogs enjoy fighting, and no correction that you can administer is likely to be severe enough to dent their enthusiasm. All you can do is concentrate on making sure that they never have the opportunity to hurt or distress someone else's pet.

Dogs communicate to each other by facial and body posture. In particular, tail carriage is a good indication of a dog's mood. Two strange male dogs will approach each other with a jaunty step, heads and tails held high. They will circle round, sniffing each other's hindquarters before breaking off the encounter to urinate on the nearest vertical surface. It appears they do this merely to indicate to other dogs that they have been there. Nervous dogs will appear smaller than they are by crouching slightly and laying their ears back. Their tails will be held tightly between their legs and they will not allow another dog to sniff their rear. The aggressive dog, on the other hand, makes itself seem larger than it is by raising the hair on the back of its neck and along its spine. This dog will be tense and stiff and it will fix its opponent with an intimidating glare. By keeping a close watch on his dog the observant owner can often be fairly sure of its next move, and may be quick enough to prevent it if it is an undesirable one.

The dog does not cool itself by sweating as we do, and indeed the few sweat glands it possesses are situated mainly in the feet. Instead, it pants. Its breath gets moister as it gets hotter and the increased evaporation from the mouth and tongue help to cool the animal down. This cooling system is only effective if the dog has plenty of air which is one of the reasons why a dog should never be left in a parked car, even if it is in a shady position. (By the time you return to the car, the sun may have moved round, so that the car is in direct sunlight.) Leaving the windows open will not be sufficient if the sun comes out, and it will also allow the dog to escape. A dog the size and shape of an Irish Setter, for example, can ease its way through an 11 cm ($4\frac{1}{2}$ in) slit if the incentive is strong enough. A parked car in strong sunlight will heat up to 120 °F, in twenty minutes or less, and any dog trapped inside would become more and more distressed and eventually lapse into a coma and die. (If you have a dog suffering from heat-stroke the most effective treatment is to submerge it in cold water up to the neck. Give it some water to drink immediately, and try to cool down its body temperature by whatever other means are available at the time.)

We are unable to explain why a dog behaves in certain ways and does many of the things it does. For example, everyone knows that a dog wags its tail when it is pleased, but why this should be a way of showing its pleasure is not known. Jumping up

Left: *Both these dogs show a confident relaxed approach to each other which indicates a willingness to make friends.*

Above right: *A Saluki invites two Norfolk Terriers to a game. Most well-adjusted dogs enjoy an energetic romp, which will seldom turn into an aggressive encounter if they are left alone.*

to greet somebody can probably be explained by natural exuberance and licking someone's hand or face in seeming affection may be traced to the maternal action of a bitch to her puppies. Other behavioural activities are less easy to explain.

The natural instincts of the dog are of varying use to man. The instinct to keep its den clean is the one that enables us to house-train the dog, while the instinct to hunt is one that the owner must control in a pet. The dog has to be taught to be selective. Chasing a ball is fun; chasing a cat is, too, but it is not allowed! The sex instinct is one that is of little use to anyone but dog breeders. As in all animals, fear is instinctive; an asset to the survival of a wild animal but often a nuisance in a pet, for nervous animals are much more difficult to train and control. The instinct to mark out a home territory with scent signals and to defend it is one that man turns to use in the guard dog. But, above all it is the pack instinct that is the greatest asset in fitting the dog into a domestic situation. Dogs are designed by nature to be team members, and as long as you make sure that you are the team leader, your dog will be a happy and willing follower.

Overleaf: *This Cairn Terrier has learnt to sit up on its hindquarters and beg for something it wants. A keen, alert, little working dog, the Cairn is one of the oldest of all Scottish breeds.*

A good worker

It turned out that Adam, who was an old man and frail, and had made some money, was going at Whitsunday to leave, and live with his son in Glasgow. We had been admiring the beauty and gentleness and perfect shape of Wylie, the finest colley I ever saw, and said, 'What are you going to do with Wylie?' 'Deed,' says he, 'I hardly ken. I canna think o'selling her, though she's worth four pound, and she'll no like the toun.' I said, 'Would you let me have her,' and Adam, looking at her fondly – she came up instantly to him, and made of him – said, 'Ay, I wull, if ye'll be gude to her,' and it was settled that when Adam left for Glasgow she should be sent into Albany Street by the carrier.

She came, and was at once taken to all our hearts – even grandmother liked her; and though she was often pensive, as if thinking of her master and her work on the hills, she made herself at home, and behaved in all respects like a lady. When out with me, if she saw sheep in the streets or road, she got quite excited, and helped the work, and was curiously useful, the being so making her wonderfully happy. And so her little life went on, never doing wrong, always blithe and kind and beautiful. But some months after she came, there was a mystery about her; every Tuesday evening she disappeared; we tried to watch her, but in vain, she was always off by nine p.m., and was away all night, back next day wearied and all over mud, as if she had travelled far. She slept all next day.

Well, one day I was walking across the Grassmarket, with Wylie at my heels, when two shepherds started, and looking at her, one said, 'That's her; that the wonderfu' wee bitch that naebody kens.' I asked him what he meant, and he told me that for months past she had made her appearance by the first daylight at the 'buchts' or sheep-pens in the cattle-market, and worked incessantly, and to excellent purpose, in helping the shepherds to get their sheep and lambs in. The man said with a sort of transport, 'She's a perfect meeracle; flees abouth like a speerit, and never gangs wrang; wears but never grups, and beats a oor dowgs. She's a perfect meeracle, and as soople as a maukin.' Then he related how they all knew her, and said, 'There's that wee fell yin; we'll get them in noo.' They tried to coax her to stop and be caught, but no, she was gentle, but off; and for many a day that 'wee fell yin' was spoken of by these rough fellows. She continued this amateur work till she died, which she did in peace.

Our Dogs by Dr John Brown
first published 1862

Index

(Figures in italics refer to illustrations)

Acknowledgments

The publishers would like to thank the following organizations and individuals for their kind permission to reproduce the photographs in this book:

Animal Graphics 4–5, 34 below left, centre and right; Ardea London (Kenneth Fink) 7 below, (Jean Paul Ferrero) 10 below, 41, 49, 50–51, 65 above right, 71, (Pat Morris) 12–13, 30; Bavaria Verlag 36, 54–55, 57, 70 above; Sdeuard C Bisserot 66; Bruce Coleman Ltd (Barry Davies) 20 above left; Anne Cumbers 15, 21, 32, 40 above, 52, 64; Daily Telegraph Colour Library (Robert Hallman) 39; Robert Estall 8 below, 27 above, 76; Mary Evans Picture Library 14 below left; Jacana Agence de Presse 13, 14 above left, 16–17, 46, 50,

53, 58 above, 68–69, 72 below right, 77 centre; Jane Miller 62–63; John Moss 9, 34 above right, 35, 38, 45, 61, 65 below right, 67; Musee de Cluny, Paris 8 above; Rex Features Ltd 24–25; Clive Sawyer 42–43 below, 60, 78; Spectrum Colour Library 56; Tony Stone Associates 26–27, 28, 29, 48, 63 below, 73; Sally-Anne Thompson 1–3, 16 below, 20 below left, 22, 23, 24 above, 44, 47, 58–59, 70 below left, 72 above left, 74–75, 77 above; Shin Yoshino 33, 69 below; Zefa 19 below, 31; Zefa/Reinhard 6–7, 18–19.

PDO 82-1039